# REENACTMENT OF A KILLER AND SERIAL RAPIST

## Cold-Eyed Mark Shirley

HELEN STOCKFORD

authorHOUSE®

*AuthorHouse™ UK*
*1663 Liberty Drive*
*Bloomington, IN 47403  USA*
*www.authorhouse.co.uk*
*Phone: 0800.197.4150*

*Published by AuthorHouse  11/28/2016*

*ISBN: 978-1-5246-3669-2 (sc)*
*ISBN: 978-1-5246-3668-5 (hc)*
*ISBN: 978-1-5246-3670-8 (e)*

*Library of Congress Control Number: 2016917748*

*Print information available on the last page.*

# CONTENTS

# DEDICATED TO MARY WAINWRIGHT

MARY …Life has shown us the ugliest form of cruelty. I am sure, in my heart, you had learnt about the two victims before you if true. That is why you eventually lost your life.

It was a sad recollection of how your life has been completely taken away by the hands of pure evil- SHIRLEY, and maybe the unfortunate souls before you. In my case, good thing my guardian angel used my son to save me, even though a huge part of me inside drastically died.

I have written this book, to enable my mind and heart to keep fighting for what is right and to pursue my candid purpose of not making such evil thrive in this world, and eventually to make a global awareness.

I hope that you Mary and all of us, whom have experienced such terror, can eventually rest.

I have thought about you always, even though I haven't met you. But I know we share the same sentiments and sorrows.

Mary, for all the other victims of Shirley- whom have remained quiet all these years, give them the strength and the courage to endure, just like you have given me.

I know in my heart you are now in a better place. As you look down on us, you will always be a guardian angel looking after my heart.

To the reader these are my exact words, a reflection of my exact narration of my story, grief, and eventually courage and how I found the strength to be resilient. This is a product of years of battle and has been written whole-heartedly.

# My Family

I know how hard it's been for you all over the last four years and for that I feel very sad and sorry.

I want you all to know how much I love you.

**Richard** you have shown me so much love and support. You could of walked away in the beginning but you didn't. You decided to stay. I want you to know how much I love you for that. I also want you to know how much I appreciate all the support you have shown.

My eldest son **SCOTT** you managed to save my life darling. From the bottom of my heart I thank you. You have shown me so much support over the last four years. You were so brave in the court. I know this has really been hard for you darling. I don't think there is anything in life that can be harder. But I want you to know that you're loved, you're very special to me.

For **Amy**, **Molly** and **Sam** you have all been through so much for that I am very sorry.

Thank you **Amy** for your support darling with different things.

I want you all to know how much mum loves you.

In time things should get better.

Thank you all

xxxx

# ACKNOWLEDGEMENT

This is a true story about a convicted murderer. **Mark Shirley** was convicted of the ritualized murder of 67 year old widow Mary Wainwright and jailed for life in 1987. After serving 16 years in prison he was released on a life licensed to attack again. Mark Shirley having been released, recalled to prison and then let out again, broke all his license rules several times especially on the 20th March 2009.

When he broke into 39 year old Helen Stockford's house, he attempted to copycat how he killed Mary Wainwright 22 years ago by sexually brutalizing Helen Stockford for five hours around her home, on her kitchen table.

Mark Shirley was found guilty of six charges those charges being: false imprisonment, committing an offence with intent to commit a sexual offence, rape and three charges of assault by penetration. He was given six life sentences with a nine year tariff so this is why I waived my name to the media because I, Helen Stockford, feel that this evil man has done far too much to me, Mary and other victims. Since 2009 Shirley has been recalled back to Bristol crown court in 2012 for an historic case dating back to 2005.

I feel Shirley should have got life with no parole! Justice has not been done as you will see when you read my story. He should not be freed to attack again he has been given lots of chances he does not deserve any more chances, as the judge said he is an evil man.

# MY LIFE WITH MY FAMILY

My name is Helen Stockford, my husband and I have been married for fifteen years. We have known each other for twenty one years. We have five children three boys and two girls. We have always had a happy marriage up and down's like most people, but our family life is normally good.

My two older sons have left school, my two daughters are at high school, and my younger son is still at primary school. I've always been a house wife, Richard has always worked he is a builder.

Everyday would be the same routine, where I would start the day with getting the kids ready for school, rushing to get my husband of to work, with a quick kiss telling him I would see him tonight.

He would always say I love you telling me to ring him if I get the chance through the day. I would take the children to school, come back home have my self a coffee, feed my animals. I would start my day with cleaning the house from top to bottom. This would take most of my time during the day. I would then prepare the food ready for the evening meal. Some women would say this life was boring, but when you love your family as much as I do, you would understand how happy and fulfilling my life was.

Evenings with my family I have always enjoyed, my children telling me about school and Richard talking about work, then they would say to me mum what have you done today and I would laugh cleaning of course!

Weekends we would do something as a family, which was always great fun, our relationship as husband and wife was very good. Richard, has always been hard working, but very caring in his own way but working very long hours through out the week. Somedays he would work twelve hours a day, but I didn't mind because we are buying our house and have lots of plans for the future together as a family.

1

We have both agreed its better to work hard now so our future can be better as we want to live abroad so that the children can have the best of most things, also as we get older we would be able to relax and be proud of what we have achieved.

Neither of us knew what was around the corner to destroy what we were building together.

# THE MEETING OF CATHY SMITH

I first met Cathy Smith in the summer of 2005. Our children at the time went to the same primary school. Cathy has two girls and one boy, her eldest daughter was in year three with my eldest daughter both girls became very close friends in school, and out of school they did ballet together.

Cathy and I, would talk in the playground. I would always talk about Richard, the house and the kids, while Cathy would talk about her work and how she would enjoy going out a lot. She never seemed settled like she didn't have enough in her life. She always seemed to be looking for something better.

I always thought this was very strange. How can someone be married, have a family and not be fulfilled. I thought, but living a very sheltered life with just Richard and the children I didn't have many friends as I have never gone to work.

The only time I would talk to people was when I was picking my children up from school or if I see my mum which would be once a day or talk to my sister's on the phone, again we would only talk about family life.

One afternoon in the playground Cathy said she was seeing someone called Nick from Sainsbury's where she worked. I said "What about your husband?"

"I want to see if I can build enough confidence if I can" she said "then I am going to divorce Darren".

As the months past her and Darren split up, she was now a single mother with three children to look after, my husband and Cathy share the same birthday. Cathy asked if we would like to go for a meal with her and Nick we said yes we would love to. I was really looking forward to going out on the 19th June 2006.

3

We had a really nice evening Nick seemed like a really nice person. A few days later Cathy said Nick had offered to pay to have her hallway decorated.

She asked me to ask Richard if he could do this for her.

Richard said "yes"

He could it took Richard about two weeks to finish the hallway. This is when our friendship really began a few weeks later Cathy started getting fed up with Nick.

She said "She felt like she had an extra child to look after, it seemed such a shame he liked the children and was a real family guy."

Cathy ended the relationship.

Poor Nick he would ring Richard.

"I don't know what I have done wrong for Cathy to do this to me."

Richard at the time felt very sorry for him, Nick felt he was used by Cathy to pay for the hallway. We felt very sad for him to be treated this way.

About a week later, Cathy said "She had met another guy at work who she liked a lot but he was in a relationship with another girl called Linda."

As the weeks past Cathy would joke on how she had been seeing Mark behind Linda's back. I told Richard and we just agreed that Cathy was just reaching out for anything and everyone. It was sad in away because I felt she was just looking for someone to love her.

Everyday all she would talk about was Mark. She said to me, "You will both have to come around with the kids and meet him" I said, "I would ask Richard."

We were introduced to Mark in the summer of 2006. He seemed ok we did notice he really didn't like Cathy's son but we said nothing as we didn't feel it was our place to tell her.

We met Mark a handfull of times at the most we did have two evenings out with them which were nice. I think Richard would get fed up sometimes because Mark would talk about how he used to get involved in lots of trouble when he was young.

A lot of things with Mark did not sort of ring true, but we didn't comment alot at the time. Then Cathy fell pregnant with Mark's baby. Cathy's family were not happy with her as Mark was still with Linda on and off plus he was still living at his flat Cathy's mother really didnt like him.

Linda found out so that was the end of their relationship. God it all seemed to be such a mess I thought to myself. Cathy would be on the phone to me alot about Mark and the way her family were treating her because of the baby having never had many friends. I felt so sorry for her. Her life had become a mess those poor children of Cathy's they didn't know what was going on in their mother's life.

A few months later, Cathy lost the baby and Mark was not with her. He was drunk in his flat; she did carry on with the relationship with Mark. It was like she could not let go of him. She loved him even though her family did not like him they would have their arguments. He would be drunk most of the time.

One evening, at Cathy's house, Mark told me and Richard "He was under probation because he was on a license", he said "It was for burglary that happened in Wales."

Cathy said. "That she was going to meet probation with Mark." If she was not back in time would I pick up the kids if she was not at school in time." thinking nothing of it, I said "yes that would be ok".

Over the next couple of months, I would only see them briefly picking up the kids from school.

A couple of times, Cathy would be on her own in the playground. I would say, how's it going and she would be cross because Mark would be at her house drunk and asleep. But even though, she would complain she still said she loved him. I would always say Cathy is this fair to the children and all she would say was their fine.

Christmas holidays 2006 Cathy and Mark called at our house for the first time, it was Christmas' eve.

Darren had the kids for a few hours so they were at a loose end and called in for a coffee. We could not offer them a proper drink as myself and Richard do not drink alcohol they stayed about an hour and then left. We had a very nice Christmas with our children we had my mum for lunch, the children played throughout the day, it was fun.

New year's eve Cathy phoned me to ask would we like to go in to town to see the New Year in together, just the four of us.

I asked Richard and said "Yes to Cathy, we had a great evening."

It was nice for me and Richard as we don't go out that much without our children. After that night I did not see Cathy until the children went back to school in January 2007.

Same day to day routine now the children were back to school and Richard back to work.

Myself and Cathy would have a chat in the playground or we would go and have a coffee if I had time. Then one day in the playground Cathy was very cross.

She said "Mark had been arrested for drink driving."

She went on to say that she had gone to work and left Mark looking after the children and that he had left the children on their own. Mark had rang her at work to say he had been stopped by the police on his bike.

I myself felt cross because of the children being left on their own but didn't get involved. By now I think I was getting fed up as here is a women that really should draw a line and think of the children.

A few days later Cathy rang me to say would I pick up her children from school as they had recalled Mark.

Cathy said. "Mark has been arrested from my house."

Richard and myself picked up the children and went straight to Cathy's house.

When we got their Cathy was very upset.

She said "Mark had been arrested for the drink driving from a few days ago", she asked Richard if he would ring the police station and find out what was going on.

The police would not tell Richard very much as he was not family. We stayed with Cathy for a few hours but could not stay the night with her because of our children she was so upset it was like her world had fallen apart and she did not know what was going on.

The following morning we took our children to school. Cathy asked us both if we wanted a coffee at her house and asked would Richard ring the police station again to find out what was going on. He rang them but again they would not tell him what was going on.

Cathy then rang probation and spoke with someone called Mathew. He told Cathy that Mark was being recalled to prison for the drink drive charge. She was told that Mark would be able to send her a visiting order once he was allowed, Cathy was so upset. Over the next few months we helped her as much as any friends would, as for her family they didn't want to know her.

Cathy got the visiting order and me and Richard went to the first prison visit to support her, but I did not like it so I did not go on a visit again.

We helped her move from her house in Filton in Bristol to the house next door to our house in Bristol.

Over the next few months, Cathy said "she was going to marry Mark in prison."

Oh my god!

I thought what is she doing! She put the wedding bands in the prison to marry him and we shopped for her dress and bridesmaid dresses. Then for some reason she said, "She was going to wait untill he was released and out of prison".

Twice a day she would write to him, she would visit him every Saturday, then she said, "She had a parole meeting to go to for Marks release this was January".

"I did offer to go with her" but she said, "No it was something she wanted to do on her own". She never said very much to me after that meeting. She was still writing to him but not as much as she was, but her visits to the prison were still every Saturday. She did not seem to be as excited as she had been in the beginning.

A few days later, we were talking in the playground about our birthdays and what we were going to do to celebrate. We agreed a girl's meal out but would meet all husbands and partners in town after.

Cathy and her friends from work, myself and my two sisters all went for a meal at TGI Fridays and then we had a limo which took us girls to town to meet our partners. I had a great time with Richard and my sisters and their husbands. Cathy's friends had a good time but Cathy left and went home, we all felt very let down because of this.

"The following day", I said, "Why did you go home?" and she said, "she was upset because Mark was not there to celebrate with her".

Cathy also ask me, "if I would go to the prison on Saturday with her just to sit outside as she had decided to finish the relationship with Mark, because she could not take the pace any longer".

I didn't really know what to say at the time, so I asked Richard and he said, "Yes if you want to so that Cathy wouldn't be on her own."

Saturday came we went to the prison and I waited outside the building for her. She was about ten minutes then she came out crying and upset.

I gave her my full support.

Richard and Cathy did have a birthday party together in a hall for their 40<sup>th</sup> birthdays. Cathy's friend, Collin, seemed really nice throughout the evening. I did think to myself how happy Cathy and her children looked and Collin seemed to be having fun with Cathy's family. As a family we didn't mention Mark.

Cathy seemed to have a good summer I didn't see much of her in the playground at school. We would have the odd coffee. She seemed happy but she still didn't look settled in herself.

Early in November 2008, Cathy asked me, "If I would look after the house and pets for the weekend. So she could go to Weymouth with her mum to close the family caravan down for the season."

I said, "Yes as I normally have the house if she goes away."

Cathy gave me the house keys, "I said have a good time we both laughed as she said, what with my mother."

When I went in the house on Friday I put all the lights on, fed the animals, closed the kitchen window and locked up on my way out.

On Saturday, I did the same thing but I did think it odd because the kitchen window was open. Strange I thought, I locked the window on my way out last night. Sunday morning I opened the front door and I thought Cathy was back as a shadow went across the top of the stairs.

I called out Cathy but nothing. So I went into the kitchen fed the cats how strange again the kitchen window was open, plus the knifes that Cathy kept by the window had been moved. It felt very creepy I felt I wasn't in the house alone, "pull yourself together" I said to myself, I locked the house and left.

Later that evening, Cathy came home she came round to mine to say, "Helen my laptop is missing."

I said, "How can it be missing?"

She said, "I don't know."

I rushed around with her thinking oh my god this looks bad, I'm the only one that has been in her house all weekend. I told Cathy how I thought she had come home early.

I told her about the window being open in the kitchen and the knives being moved. I felt sick and dizzy.

"I have never stolen anything in my life", I said to Cathy, and she said, "I know that silly."

"Ring the police" I said to Cathy, and her mother had told her the same.

The police came but they found nothing, Cathy's family firmly believed I had stolen the laptop. As for me it made me feel ill and very embarrassed, me and Cathy didn't bother with one another because of her family and mine.

We would greet each other "Hi!" and that was all our friendship had finished. I felt very let down after everything me and my husband had done for her and her children. As for my older daughter she felt very hurt that Cathy's family could think such a thing of her mum.

I felt very sad deep down as I couldn't account for that weekend the laptop went missing, also because Cathy didn't stand up to her family over me. I missed Cathy's children very much and would worry about Cathy because she lived on her own.

I didn't think our friendship would come to an end like this I felt very hurt. We did manage to have a very small Christmas drink together which was nice, but I felt very uncomfortable in Cathy's house.

# THE DAYS LEADING UP
# TO THE ATTACK

We hadn't seen or heard anything about Mark Shirley since the summer of 2008 when Cathy broke up with him at the prison.

I had not seen much of Cathy over the following months as with the laptop going missing from her house it put a wedge between the two families.

On the 12th March 2009, we were out shopping. When we got back at 7.45pm, Mark Shirley was crouched down by the side of our front door step. Straight away as I was coming up the pathway with Richard and the children, I said "What are you doing here Mark?" and "why are you crouched down there?"

Mark replied "I've just come to let you both know that I have spoken with Cathy, and she's agreed

I can pick up my motor bike from her back garden tomorrow. So I thought I would come and let you both know as I didn't want you to think I'd broken in next door."

We told Mark that it had nothing to do with us. I did tell him not to call again at the house as I didn't want bad feelings with Cathy next door.

Richard and Mark had a chat in the hallway, as Mark had been drinking and I didn't want him around my children. Poor Richard he had to listen to Mark for about half an hour, he was talking about his love for Cathy and how Cathy had hurt him.

He was drunk which made it worse as Richard didn't really know what to say to him. Richard told Mark that he would sort out the few boxes we had of his in our loft.

Richard said, "He would get them out and drop them down to him."

Mark was happy with that arrangement, Richard and Mark then said their goodbyes.

Later that evening, Cathy text me to say she had spoken with Mark and he was getting his motorbike tomorrow morning.

I text back saying, Yes, we know as Mark called to our house Cathy. I told her, what I had told Mark it's nothing to do with us.

The following morning on the 13th of March 2009, Richard went to work. I took the children to school just a normal day, as I was cleaning the kitchen and the conservatory. Mark gave a small waive from Cathy's back garden he had someone with him.

I gave a small waive back and thought I will give him some privacy so I pulled my blinds down slightly.

As the day went on I didn't think any more of it. Cathy text me later that day to say, Mark couldn't move the bike as it was broken so he has to get a van to move it. I didn't text back.

# The Day Mark Shirley
# Broke Into My House

## FRIDAY 20TH MARCH 2009

The day started like another normal day. Richard left for work I took the children to school. I was back home by ten past eight, made my coffee and sorted the animals out locked up the house and started the cleaning upstairs.

Around 8.40am I came down stairs my kitchen and dinning room are open plan leading onto my conservatory. I noticed, as I walked through my living room, that it was really dark. My blinds were pulled down. How strange, I thought we never touch the blinds.

As I walked through, I noticed Mark Shirley sat at the end of my long farm house kitchen table on a chair. "God my blood froze," "how did you get in Mark?" I asked.

I looked at his face his skin was a terrible grey colour and he stank of alcohol his eyes were just staring at me.

It was like looking at a completely different person. I had once met through Cathy. My voice felt tight as I asked him again

"What are you doing here Mark?"

"How did you get in?"

Mark struggled with his words, "I did knock you didn't hear me?" he said.

I then said, "Well, how did you get in?"

Mark just looked at me and said, "I thought I'd just pop in for a coffee" when I asked him, Why he had pulled my blinds down, He just grinned at me that hideous look and smile scared me more than ever.

Fighting to keep control of myself I told him that he had to leave as I had to go out.

That's when he snapped at me (sit down) he looked so menacing I was scared.

I did not dare argue with him. He then got up off his chair he was sat on and he made himself a coffee he then sat back at the table with his coffee.

Mark began saying, "He once knew a lovely lady who's name was Mary" he said.

He stalked her for weeks through her washing line he said she lived in a flat in Wales.

Mark began saying, "Because she looked a lovely trustable lady, he broke into her flat and put her through so much pain. He felt she trusted him."

He went on to say that, "I looked a very lovely trusting lady just like Mary."

I felt sick with fear. I said, "I dont know Mark,"

He then got upset and very angry with me. He said, "You should know she lives in Wales".

"Mark" I said, "I do not know who Mary is?"

I then said, "Would you like me to take you there in my car, thinking hopefully he would agree."

Mark got up from his chair with me still talking to him telling him he would have to guide me to the place in Wales. We got half way through my living room when Mark had a change of heart and grabbed me round my mouth pulling me back into the kitchen telling me that I was just trying to trick him.

Mark then got upset. "I'm going to make you smell as sweet as Mary", he said, "pushing me back on the chair."

My blood ran cold I knew in that instant, in his mind it did look like I was trying to trick him even though I was just thinking of a way out of the house to get some help.

He then leaned over the chair where I was sat and he pulled out a flick knife from the waist band of his jogging bottoms and started to order me to take my arms out of my black top.

He started brandishing the knife over the top half of my body."

"I'm going to make you smell as sweet as Mary," he started cutting pieces from my bra so my nipples were bare; he then cut my bra through the middle so he could touch and smell my bare skin."

"Mark you are scaring me just leave the house," I said.

"No one needs to know you were here please" Mark I said, "I dont show my body to anyone,"

"I love Richard, Mark please leave."

He whispered, "Richard will understand, trust me Mary."

"Im going to make you smell sweet again, you are so warm and soft," he said.

"It was then that I knew I had become Mary in his twisted mind I felt sick with terror, self preservation kicked in. I knew I would have to do anything-however disgusting and degrading it might be to stay alive.

"He ordered me to get up on the kitchen table where he stripped me of my clothes over and over he called me Mary running the knife over my body and putting it in my private areas.

I was thinking please God let me pick my children up today please dont let him kill me.

I felt like I was on an operating table waiting for the first cut.

Mark ordered me off the table.

"He dragged me through the living room by my neck and my hair. He started pulling me up the stairway because I was very unsteady. He was laughing at me and telling me that I was an angel just like many others."

He ordered me to stay on the landing. He went into my daughter's bedroom and through their clothes when he came out from the bedroom onto the landing he started dressing me in child's underwear he was laughing as he was pulling the knickers on me.

He started smelling my skin pulling at the knickers to lick and smell my privates.

He started talking about his first angel how she had soft skin and lovely hair laughing to himself saying she had lent him ten pence for the tuck shop at youth-club as his stepdad hadn't given him any sweet money.

Still pulling at the underwear Mark dressed me in, Mark started to tell me how he had later started to walk the girl home from youth club. Mark told me how he had tried to kiss her, Mark then started to laugh out loud, saying she made me angry, so I put my jacket over her head and pulled her into a shed. Mark was pulling at my hair when he was saying all this.

Putting his face into mine he shouted "she had started to smell not nice 'pulling me across the landing'. He was telling me how she made him wait untill it got dark and no one was around. He said "He managed to carry her into the fields at the back of the houses where he lived."

Mark was laughing but at the same time he was very angry shouting, "You stupid pure angel."

"I had to hide you under loads of leaves; you thought you were better than me?" "Didn't you?" he cried.

"I'm only fourteen you made me put my cock inside you and my pocket knife", he laughed my red pocket penknife wasted on a pure angel.

Moments later, "he pulled the underwear of me", and said, "She was a little angel that made him very angry."

"As I watched him shout and cry I really didn't know what to do. I didn't know whether to talk or try to move I felt embarrassed and hurt. I was terrified of him plus I was terrified because I knew I was overlooking the stairway."

"Mark Shirley, walked in to my bedroom and laid on my bed laughing. I could hear him saying angels, fucking angels everywhere he started walking around my bedroom going through cupboards and our wardrobes."

"I could not see much of what he was doing, when he came back on the landing he had a few of my underwear outfits, putting the outfits up against me and smelling me he started to lick my private areas. He started to dress me in the outfit of his choice, dressing me in one that he liked he started telling me what his home town was like."

"I felt very sick and scared, he kept shouting at me because I didn't know what to say."

"Smelling and touching my body was really killing me deep down inside every time he put his fingers inside me and his mouth near I just wanted to die."

Telling me I smelt really sweet he called me by another name but I can't remember the name as he said it and laughed really loud."

"Pushing me over the handrail he got really angry he put both hands inside me really hard shouting "I'm only fifteen you fucking horrible angel." "Find it funny do you"

Mark Shirley started shouting and crying gripping me very tight telling me: "what nice young skin and hair this person had" he said, "he needed to fuck her hard just like jiffy the babysitter had showed him when he was 12 he pulled me of the banister rail by my hair and sad they were both innocent and pure but they made me angry" he cried.

My body was really sore my head was banging I felt really dizzy from being over the hand rail. I just wanted him to leave my house.

Moments later Mark Shirley started to dress me in another outfit of mine, as he was dressing me he started to say "you're such a trusted lady Mary" laughing and talking about his friends.

I can remember that one was called Billy, there were more but I can't remember them.

He told me how they all hung out in patchway and Filton area there were more areas but I don't remember them all, great fun he laughed it was almost like he was having fun.

I daren't look at him as I'm too scared he grabbed me and shook me saying "I've fancied you for a few weeks another pretty fucking angel, you made me very fucking angry so I had to learn you a lesson" (shaking inside).

"He ripped my underwear of me saying how glad he was that he fucked and hurt her hard, putting his fingers inside me and sucking my breast he started laughing, "the only thing you had going for you was your skin smelt nice" putting his face in mine.

Mark Shirley said "hurting you hard I know you won't tell you're a sad sad angel, no one will want you now but at least I still hang with my girlfriend and mates" he laugh taking his face away from mine.

I felt really sick and scared, pulling his fingers out really hurt me but he just laughed, Mark Shirley then sat himself on the floor.

"My trusted angel Mary, sit down with me." Mark said.

"I was feeling very dizzy and not well so I just sat down. I felt very ashamed as I had nothing on but I didn't know what else to do."

Mark Shirley started to cry, "you do understand me don't you Mary?" Mark said.

I replied "Yes!" as I was very scared.

"I felt so ill I felt confused. Mark Shirley started telling me that he liked going out with his mates drinking and taking drugs with my mates is good fun.

He started laughing "You do understand me Mary don't you?"

I replied "Yes I think so."

"Mary walking home late is very hard," he started shouting "Yea angels Mary I've had two or three more since you I make them smell nice like you Mary, I grab them from behind so they can't see me Mary!"

"I fuck them hard Mary and tell them not to move or I'd use my knife on them. They had nice hair and soft skin my breath was on them he shouted just like the other angels and you Mary.

I always leave them face down on the grass", Mark Shirley started to cry "they made me angry Mary just like the others", Mark Shirley started to laugh, "Mary it was funny I watched the police for a few weeks they were asking people to come forward, you do understand me Mary don't you?"

I didn't reply so he shook me and said, "They weren't pure angels Mary but they made me angry", Mark then told me to get up.

"By one arm Mark Shirley, started pulling me down the stairway, the experience was horrible he pulled me by my hair into the bathroom. I felt very ashamed as I was naked pulling me by my hair. I had to give him a shower to clean the angels away I felt dizzy and sick."

"Mark Shirley made me have oral sex with him in the bathroom I had to please him, he put a shampoo bottle inside me as I leant over the sink the pain was awful, he put toothpaste on a tooth brush and scrubbed my bottom he put his fingers inside me it really felt like I was going to die."

"I felt so ashamed as I had no control, he kept laughing and laughing telling Mary how warm and good she felt."

"Mark Shirley tried to put a hair brush inside me as he wanted Mary to bleed, as the hair brush went in my private area. I remember feeling dizzy and having a sharp pain."

I remember saying "Stop Mark you are hurting me".

"I know I fell down the next thing I remember is I'm back on the kitchen table, Mark was moving me around.

He had a ruck sack with him which was by the side of the freezer from the view. I had from the table, it had a few knifes and what looked like a circular cutter and a jumper. God I was feeling so scared it was like everything was in a daze."

"I knew in my heart the contence of the rucksack was meant for hurting and killing me.

All the time Mark was pulling me around the table putting my body in different positions there were points when my breasts had to hang over the table."

"Mark was angry with me because my body kept shaking I could not control my head he kept maniacally muttering to himself that he had to work out which way he should cut me and which way he wanted the blood to flow, so that I would smell as sweet as Mary."

My stomach churned when he told me to keep very still or like Mary he would take my face off. Mark raped me four times and he abused me with his knife.

"I cannot describe the agony he then layed on top of me and sniffed my skin covering me in my own mess telling me that Fridays and Saturdays are his good killing days he murmured "Mary I killed on Friday.

"I felt sickened and humiliated having this monster on my body and smelling me all over I really began to feel what he had put Mary through as he was doing the same to me."

"One moment he was sobbing the next he was laughing maniacally then he started ranting to himself and tipping his rucksack inside out looking for a two pence piece and a knife.

"This really scared me as he was looking to leave these items on my body if he kills me that was what he left on Marys body to make her look pretty he also said he covered part of her body with a cloth to try and keep her warm and soak up her blood.

"It became clear he'd planned to do the same to me but he couldn't find the coin he had brought with him, perhaps that brought me time I dont know I am in absolutely no doubt that Mark wants to kill me."

"I kept very still as still as I could which is very hard when you are terrified thinking god Im not going to pick the kids up they are going to come home to find me dead.

"From a distance I heard someone shouting mum and banging on my conservatory doors Mark froze he paniced he grabbed my clothes and started to dress me my body felt like lead I was so frightened my knees buckled and I crashed to the kitchen floor."

"Mark Shirley forced me to my feet and pushed me towards the doors. I dont know how I let my son in. I must have been so traumatised at the time I watched as Mark Shirley greeted my son so cheerfully it was utterly horrific.

His demenour was so cool and I was so traumatised my son didn't notice this man was about to kill his mum just before he arrived, I remember Scott saying, "what are you doing here mate? Mum doesn't have anyone in when dads at work".

Mark said "I just called in for a coffee mate and to let mum know I've contacted Cathy about my bike which was still at Cathy's in her back garden."

"Scott then took himself in to the living room with his bag of chips and put TV on. Mark Shirley kicked my foot under the table and told me to see him out properly. I walked Mark Shirley through my living room in to the hallway, my head and heart was thumping.

I was in a total daze, Mark Shirley grabbed my face and whispered "if you tell anyone whats happened I will come back and kill you and your daughters" he also handed me my mobile phone and said "he'd covered his tracks by texting himself through out the attack."

He said "he should of killed me when he took the laptop from Cathy's. Yes- he grinned, I was in the house. He kissed me on my left cheek and left my house.

Afterwards when I came back in from the hallway I sat back on the kitchen chair I must of gone into autopilot, Scott started telling me about his day. I can honestly say I can't remember a word. Somehow I must of managed to nod in all the right places but my mind was trapped in the nightmare I'd just lived through.

Five hours is a long time, especially when your waiting to be killed. Even when Richard came home at 3pm I managed to greet him as normal as possible. I even managed to pick my children up from school in the same clothes I'd been attacked in, still covered in all the mess on my skin and with the cut bra in my jean pocket. It was almost like an out of body experience, I was looking down at myself going over all the motions of the day.

# THE FOLLOWING COUPLE OF DAYS

"Incredible as it seems for the next few days I lived with this terrible secret. I didn't tell anyone, not my husband not even the police as I was frozen with fear and shock.

"From the Friday untill the Sunday Mark kept texting my phone warning me not to talk or he would kill me, he even went as far as wishing me a Happy Mother's Day."

"Richard could not understand why my mobile phone was so busy and he couldn't understand why I cringed every time he came near me and snapped at the slightest thing.

We went shopping on the Saturday to Asda we had an argument because I wasn't shopping like I normally would, poor Richard I was not copeing very well but I didn't want him to know as it felt like Mark Shirley's last words were still with me.

"Apart from the shopping I spent the rest of the weekend sat alone on my garden step, it felt like my family was so far away.

"When the house was silent at night I would just go to the bathroom and scrub and scrub, my skin was sore but I didn't feel clean, I washed the clothes I had on time and time again but I put the clothes in a bag under the stairs so my family would not find them.

I just didn't know what to do with myself; my head didn't want to think. I just felt numb.

# On Monday 23ʳᵈ March 2009

My family got up, everyone rushing to get ready for work and school, me myself was doing everything. I normally would do but it seemed like I was doing it all at a very slow pace. Thinking god Ive got to go to school on my own, would Mark be out there just waiting to kill me.

I dont want Richard to go to work. Well I managed to pull myself together Richard left for work I made it to school with my children even though I was trying to hurry them all because I didn't feel safe.

When I pulled up outside my house in my car Cathy was in her driveway and said, "Helen can you spare sometime please."

"What for Cathy" I said.

"Ive had some funny texts from Mark over the weekend, Cathy said

She needed to contact probation to report Mark." My heart just stopped with fear, but I said "yes but I couldn't stay long" and she said, "that's fine thank you".

Cathy made a coffee which I really didn't want and she then rang probation. Cathy told probation that I could confirm Mark had been in contact with her, they then asked to speak to me.

When Cathy handed me the phone I heard a ladys voice she said "Hi Helen, Im Fiona Burch can you confirm what Cathy is telling me", (straight away I don't know why but) I asked, "Can you please tell me, did Mark deface Mary I need to know."

I cried, I pleaded and pleaded, "I need to know'.

Cathy grabbed the phone and I just broke down. Fiona stayed on the phone and told Cathy to lock the doors and phone the police.

I was so terrified, I felt so dirty and ashamed. Cathy took me to Southmead police station. Cathy tried to explain on the front desk.

By now I was just a mess I couldn't think straight terrified they might not believe me.

They put myself and Cathy in a side room. "I can't face or tell a man" I said.

Cathy asked for a lady officer. P.C Ham came into the room it was hard but I tried to tell her what had happened but didn't tell her everything as I was very scared.

Cathy explained, "Mark was on probation with a life lience" P.C Ham said she would contact Helen when she had spoken with her Sergeant and probation.

On my way back from the police station, I started to panic. God what have I done Mark's coming back for me or my daughters, hes going to kill us. I wish Cathy hadn't of asked me into her house this morning as then no one would know. I told Cathy I wanted to go into my house to be alone Cathy said "Ok, lock your doors".

Cathy then said "Helen, I will come round your house if anyone rings, i.e. the police or probation." I just replied "Ok thanks Cathy".

When I was alone, I just sat down thinking I need to talk to Richard. Crying and feeling very scared, I rang Richard's mobile he answered and said, "Hi babe what's up?" I replied. "Nothing, I just needed to hear your voice, but there's something I need to tell you".

Richard replied "Babe what's wrong?", "nothing" I said, "I will see you later, try not to be home too late". He replied, "I was packing up now anyway and will be home soon".

I sat for a while just feeling very ashamed and dirty, it was like I didn't know what to do. I just kept thinking what if Richard finds out he might leave me or he might hunt down Mark. How am I going to tell him what Mark has done to me in our house.

Cathy came round to my house to check if I was ok, Cathy said "Helen, Fiona Burch from probation has just rang me back. "What has Fiona said Cathy" I asked. Cathy continued, "Helen she has told me to inform you that Mark is going to be recalled, but Helen, Fiona has told me to tell you that it won't be today! As they need to sort all the paperwork first for Mark Shirley's arrest. Helen I have also spoken with the police to ask them if they can take a statement and they have told me to tell you, Helen they will phone you when PC Ham is back on duty." "Ok" I replied. Cathy then replies "Helen I've also told the police about probation and what Fiona had told me to tell you. "Ok" I replied. Cathy continues "Helen, the police have told me to tell you not to worry and keep yourself locked indoors, as they cannot secure your house at this stage! I don't think I thanked Cathy at this stage as I was very terrified and lost for words.

By Cathy telling me all this information it made me feel even more terrified. Why aren't the police helping me right now, I thought.

Richard came home around 5pm when he came in he said "sorry I'm a bit late babe, I was coming along Southmead road and Mark flagged me over. We have been chatting about his bike". I just felt dizzy Richard said, "What's wrong". I just stood there looking at him. Richard I said, "Mark broke into our house last Friday and done things he should not have done. Im waiting for the police to ring me".

"What do you mean Helen?" Richard shouted. "I'm going to kill him!" Richard headed straight for the front door, just as Cathy was coming into our house. Cathy took Richard outside the house to talk with him.

When they came in Richard said, "Mark made arrangements for him to go to his flat for coffee at 9.30pm tonight". We both told Richard he couldn't because the police were dealing with Mark and probation are re-calling him as soon as they sort the paper work out. Cathy went home. Richard kept saying he wanted to go to Marks at 9.30pm.

I told Richard, "You can't let's wait for the police to ring", he didn't look happy. I felt so sad and hurt because I couldn't tell him what Mark had really done.

I feel so ashamed why didn't Mark just kill me I kept thinking. Richard and I are normally very close but I felt very distant looking at Richard I could see his head was just going around with, "Why did Mark break in our house and what's he done", he kept saying "What's Mark done Helen", it was a very long night for us both.

# Tuesday 24ᵗʰ March 2009

Richard asked if I wanted him to stay at home from work. I snapped back saying, "no go to work.' Richard said "Babe, I'm really worried about you. Please babe you need me home you look very unwell".

I said, "No go to work Im fine".

Richard just got in his car and went when he left I managed to take the children to school with Cathy. I kept looking around myself thinking god if Mark sees me with Cathy then he will kill me.

When I got back I rang the police to ask if P.C. Ham was on duty they told me she would ring me sometime today, they said they still couldn't secure the house untill they knew they had grounds to do so.

Cathy called a lock smith and had the door locks changed on both houses. We both then stayed in our own houses locked in not that it made any difference, I knew Mark was still out there.

Richard kept ringing to see if I was ok around about lunchtime. I was talking to Richard on the phone, Cathy texts me to say she was coming around. I unlocked the front door and let her in. She said, "Helen, its ok they have just rang me to say that they have detained Mark".

I instantly felt sick and my legs just buckled beneath me, silent tears rolled down my face. Cathy said "Helen its ok, Mark is detained now Fiona has told me to tell you to try not to worry the police will be contacting you very soon. I replied "ok, thank you Cathy."

A few hours later I spoke with the police and they told me they didn't know when they were going to see me but it would be this week when P.C Ham could fit me in with her shifts.

This left me feeling that nothing was being done. I thought they would of wanted a statement and to have the clothes. I wore that day as a family we had a very bad evening we just didn't no what was going on with the police.

I was feeling very tired and my body was very sore. I really just didn't want to be around Richard and the children. I felt like I was sitting under thick black fog and couldn't see out.

# *Wednesday 25ᵗʰ March 2009*

On the 25ᵗʰ March after having a really bad night I got up really feeling unwell. I managed to get Richard off to work. I felt really sad for him as he looked so confused and pale but there was a part of me that was trying to keep the normal routine because I didnt want the children to suffer. It's a very strange feeling!

You just feel that you are in a world completely on your own not knowing where to turn or what to do.

You want to reach out to loved ones but you can't you feel too ashamed and dirty.

Around about late morning I had a phone call from the police. "Mrs. Stockford we are sending someone round to secure your house". "Thank you", I replied. When I put the phone down I remembered thinking to myself, they are sending a work man round. I froze they can't I cryed to myself, I can't have a man in my house.

I managed to give in to my feelings and rang Richard, "I need you to come home Richard they are sending someone round to secure the house. I can't deal with this on my own". He said "calm down I will see you shortly ok".

Within about an hour of Richard being home they arrived to secure the house. I just sat and watched as they locked my windows, my letter box had to be secured, they changed the door locks they put alarms on my windows and doors plus they gave Richard personal alarms for me and my two daughters.

I could feel Richard looking at me with as much to say, what is going on we've only had a break in. I just looked around myself feeling totally traumatized and ashamed for the rest of the day and evening I sat in silence and just kept falling asleep in between this I kept thinking about Mary did she really die like he said or was he just trying to scare me.

I kept thinking did he really take her face off in temper, and all the blood talk was Mark telling the truth, god I kept thinking it can't be true. I tried to go over what he had done to me but I couldn't because I was confused about Mary and all the things Mark had said.

In my mind I would keep saying, why Mark it would have been better if you had of killed me.

On the 26th March 2009, same routine with a struggle I asked Cathy if she would take me to the police station as I really knew in my head that I wouldn't take the pace of another day just waiting for them to ring me.

When we got to the police station the lady on the desk said, "P.C Ham wasn't on shift untill 10pm that evening but she would see if I was allowed to come in at that time to make my statement. "Go home Mrs Stockford and we will ring you."

After about two hours they rang to say that was fine thay would see me at 10pm the rest of the day and early evening went very long. I just feel so wore out. When I arrived at the police station P.C Ham took me and Cathy in a back room as the hours past. I managed to give P.C Ham a full statement of what happened on the 20th March 2009 when Mark Shirley broke into my house.

She kept saying, "Helen shall we take a break" and I kept telling her, "no" for some reason.

I felt I just had to tell her what this man had done. P.C Ham said, "Helen we have to stop now", she took my carrier bag with the clothes inside and said, "Helen Im really sorry I didn't realise it was so bad.

When you came in on Monday I thought I was just dealing with an ordinary break in", at that point I said to her, "but he was arrested on Tuesday", "yes" she said "but he doesn't think hes been arrested for this, he thinks it's for the texts messages he sent Cathy".

"Helen Im going to have to speak to my Sergeant as this statement is to involved for me my darling", "ok" I said when she came back in to the room she said "Helen my Sergeant has sent it straight up to CID".

I just sat there and cried, "don't be frightened darling CID are very experienced. Go home and get some rest, your not alone now", she said, "they will ring you Helen try not to worry".

We got back home about 3.30am. Richard was asleep on the sofa when I came in I just sat on the rug in the living room looking at him he looked so peaceful. I just cried silent tears why has this happened to me, my poor family they are going to be so shocked and hurt when they learn the truth, I really felt like I wanted to die.

LIVING ROOM LEADING TO THE KITCHEN

TOP END OF KITCHEN WHERE MARK HELPED
HIMSELF TO COFFEE THROUGHOUT THE DAY

THIS IS THE CONSEVATORY AREA PATIO DOOR'S TO
THE SIDE WHERE I MANAGED TO LET MY SON IN.

# LIVING IN THE HANDS OF CID

## FRIDAY 27TH MARCH 2009

I had a phone call from CID, Liz Coles, to say could her and a work partner come to the house to see me as P.C. Ham had sent my statement through to her department I said, "Yes that would be fine". Liz said, "They would be around about 1.00pm".

When the two officers arrived one was called Liz and the other was called Deb's they explained what sort of work they both covered. I found them to be very nice and very understanding.

We spoke for quite a while debs said, "We will do everything at your pace Helen as we know how hard this is going to be for you and your family".

I then cryed and said, "My husband Richard doesn't know much", "dont worry" they said, "we will help you with telling him". They then went on to say that they would need my mobile phone plus my boots.

I had on as I wore them on the day of the attack they said that their sargent would need his team of forensic's to come into the house to look for dna of Marks plus any prints he may of left behind.

I said, "When would this need to be done". Liz said, "Today as it was going to take a couple of days. Helen have you got any where that you and Richard could take the children for the weekend".

I cried and said, "No plus I can't today as my little girls Amy and Molly have their party hall booked and all their friends are being picked up from school in limo's and a few are sleeping over tonight", Debs said, "Ok calm down Im sure we can sort this out together so that we can try and keep it normal for the children without them getting upset".

I said, "Ok thank you".

Liz said, "Helen we are just going off to buy you a cheap phone. You make yourself a drink and stay calm until we get back. We won't be long".

I rang Richard to ask him to come home and he said, "Im on my way home darling".

When the two CID officers came back to my house, they had some brown paper bag with them. They explained the bags were for my boots and mobile phone.

Richard came home Liz and Debs introduced themselves to him they explained to Richard that they had got me a new phone and that their sargent would need the house over the weekend, they explained to Richard that Debs would be working for him and our son Scott as she would need statements from them both about Mark.

She also asked Richard if he had anything on his phone from Mark he said, "Yes a couple of texts messages".

She said, "They would have to take his phone for evidence as well Debs told Richard that I had been raped and attacked by Mark but she couldn't give him ant details as Richard had to be a witness because he had seen Mark on the Monday and I had to stay pure for the trial.

Richard was devastated and shocked. I asked the two officers if Mark Shirley had told me the truth about Mary. Liz replied "Helen, the most we can tell you is that Mark Shirley has got a past history, but we can't tell you anything else Helen. I'm very sorry".

"Helen", Liz said "we need to sort out what we are going to do with the house" they said that they had spoken to their sargent and he was happy to start with his team on Saturday morning but it would have to be early.

We rang around the parents and made arrangements for them all to be picked up by 9.30am. I felt so ill I didn't really want this childrens party but it had been booked for months and I didn't want to let my daughters down.

Liz said, "We will keep ringing you Helen just to make sure your ok".

I felt so confussed about everything at this point Richard took me to the doctors who were very understanding and they put me on diazipan tablets to calm me down.

Myself and Richard, then went to the birthday hall after the doctors to trim up the hall and put the party food out, poor Richard he had done more than me and yet he looked terrible and very pale indeed.

We didn't know what to say to each other Richard was trying so hard to comfort me but I couldn't lean on him. This big part of me kept shying away from him.

Liz phoned to confirm that the Sergeant was fine with the arrangements but did stress that we kept the kitchen and consevatory area closed up and didn't use it from now on.

The children arrived at the hall all laughing about what fun they had in the fire engine limo's my sister Mandy arrived and I managed to tell her what had happened. She was so hurt and yet she put a brave face on and really helped me give those kids a good time she was the only one that helped Richard.

At the end of the evening she helped Richard get the children in the car and took them home. When Richard came back up to the hall for me and a few more children he looked very strange like he wanted to say something but didn't know how.

As we pulled into the street where we lived I could see police cars everywhere "Richard", I said, "what is going on in our street" he said, "try not to panic the house is under surveillance".

I broke down in tears "what about the children" I said, "they know nothing and their friends".

In the house my sister Mandy just held me. I said to her "why has this happened to me?" and she said "I dont know love, come on" she said "we will get through it together".

"Why didn't he just kill me Mandy?".

"I just dont want to be here anymore". "Come on dont talk like that" Mandy said.

"Life wouldn't be the same without you come on sort your self out as we have got to do the children".

"I can't face my children or Richard, this is all my fault". Mandy replied "No it's not your fault you didn't invite this man into your house." I said "I know that but I don't know what to do.

Mandy said, "well then he is in the wrong not you but he should of done this to Cathy next door shes the one that was going to marry him she was the one that hurt him by breaking up with him" Mandy said, "I know love".

Together we managed to sort the children out and put them to bed, Richard managed to sort everything out with the police.

The police agreed they would move their cars in the morning, so parents could park at my address to pick up their children. Also because we didn't want all the parents to see the police at our house.

It was a very long night Richard didn't sleep. I did manage to get an hour on the sofa but had some terrible dreams.

# Saturday 28<sup>th</sup> March 2009

I woke up early my body feeling very bruised and sore I said to Richard, "are the police still outside", "yes" he said, "what are we going to do with the kids Richard it's our daughter 13<sup>th</sup> birthday we have no where to take them for the weekend", I made me and Richard a hot drink. Richard said, "Helen, don't worry I'm sure your mum will help us with our children" I replied, "ok I will try and call her when we have finished our drinks."

I rang my mother who lives in the next street to where our house is situated. On talking to my mum she could not understand anything of what was going on. It was so hard as I wasn't allowed to tell my mother to much as CID had told me I was not allowed to discuss anything with my family.

I asked my mother if she could have the children at her house, while I tried to sort things out. My mother replied "yes but she could not have them for long as she was going out"

This made me feel very alone I felt like saying I need you mum but I was not brave enough. Around 8.45am the police started to move away from the house slightly so that the parents could park and pick up their daughters.

Once all the children had gone. I told my children that they had to go to nannys house so they needed to get ready. Our daughter Amy looked sad because it was her birthday.

I didn't know what to tell them they looked so confused. Richard took them around to my mums and said, "We would pick them up in about an hour" my mum said, "that would be ok".

When Richard returned CID Liz and Debs and others arrived at our house and came in.

Liz said, "This is what is going to happen today Helen the forensic team will be working right the way through the day and night untill early hours of the morning and I would imagine and then tomorrow another team will come in and clean and put everything in the house back to normal".

Liz said, "We have managed to get you and Richard a hotel for tonight but not for the children. Is there anyone that can have them for you", I said "I would try and ask my mum".

I did say to Liz what about my animals they were very understanding and they agreed that we could come back early evening to feed them and make sure they were ok.

We didn't see Cathy and she didn't offer to help with the kids or the animals I felt very hurt as there was no one we could turn to for help.

We went to my mum's house and picked up the children it was a very long day for them just driving around not knowing what to do. We sat in the Burger King Restaurant for a while honestly it was like I was having a nightmare but I was awake.

My children at around 5pm looked so fed up I rang my mum to ask could she have them over night as I had nowhere to take them.

I explained that the police had got me and Richard a hotel but not for the children I also told her I just could not manage them. She said, "It was fine", so I dropped them off on the understanding they were not allowed to go around to our house I didnt want them to see what was going on there.

Once I had dropped them off we went round to our own house to see if the animals were ok, their were a few ferenzic vans parked outside my house and across the other side of the pavement a police car was still sitting by my house.

I was dreading walking through my own front door when I did I felt so sick to my stomach as my home had been tipped upside down there were all these people in white suits spreading black dust and taking prints all over the place.

My kitchen table and chairs were wrapped up in brown paper ready to be taken away my dinner plates and cups and cutlery were put in bags ready to be taken away, my blinds in the consevatory had no cords on them they were in bags ready to be taken away and as I walked through I noticed a trainer print on my kitchen floor which I knew was not one of ours this print just made me feel sick and so upset and hurt because I just knew it was Marks shoe print.

It was down by where the rucksack was placed on the day of the attack I just looked around and didn't know what to think or feel I managed to feed the animals with the police saying, "try not to touch anything Helen please".

They said they needed Richard to give them a hand with some of the stuff, Richard looked very worried for me he said, "Babe go and have a coffee with Cathy while I give the police a hand". I didn't really want to go but I felt I could not watch as they were taking the table out Richard stayed to help them.

About an hour later Richard text me to say he had finished, thank God I thought as I didn't feel well in Cathy's house, plus I felt this should be happening to her not me and my family plus it felt, by the way Cathy was talking she was the victim not me. I just felt sick and needed to leave her house.

Before I left to go to the hotel they showed me my panic button box they had fitted and how to use it the police told Richard they would ring when they were finished for the night.

We went to the hotel which was terrible for me as I just felt terrified and scared. I just couldn't rest I was worried about my children.

I kept thinking about my house which was my home even though it didn't feel like home anymore and my poor dogs they had been in the rain all day.

A few hours went by the police phoned to say that they had finished for the night and they would be back in the morning to clean up, they said the police were still going to stay outside the house over night Richard said, "ok thank you" the call then ended.

I couldn't rest so Richard took me home for a bit the house was so dirty and it felt cold it looked so empty without my big farm house table and chairs I was so upset.

"When is this going to end" I cried Richard just comforted me and said "dont worry babe Im here".

At about 5.30am we went back to the hotel Richard made me lay down and rest about 7am. I had a shower and Richard went and got breakfast delivered in our room.

I didn't eat very much but I had a little bit as I had not eaten for days and Richard was worried about me. We left the hotel at 8am and headed home as I wanted to clean the house and get my children back home where they belonged.

# *Sunday 29th March 2009*

I was cleaning the house when CID arrived, "you dont have to do that Helen the cleaners will be here shortly to do that".

I snapped at Liz and said to her, "I want to clean my house". I think mentally I just needed to feel like I was putting the house back together for the children so that they would not suffer with the house looking like it did.

The cleaners arrived and came in they explained what they were going to do and then started to remove all the black dust from around the house.

I was just going behind them cleaning how I would normally clean my house as I didnt feel it was as clean as I would do it.

Liz and Debs said to me, "We are going off to get you a new table and chairs Helen so the children don't notice too much".

I said, "thank you".

They were gone a few hours the house was starting to look clean.

As my children came home Liz and Debs arrived back, I must say in front of the children they both had a great sense of humor they joked about how they got mums new table and chairs in their small car they also joked with the children when it came to dad putting the table together.

I was feeling so up in the air and feeling really ill but I was greatful to them both for what they did.

Liz also said that they were going to put Richard on leave for two weeks from work to begin with so he could try and get to grips with what had happened.

When they left Liz turned to me and said, "Helen you can ring us when ever you need to if not we will ring you", Debs went to my mums to take a statement from Scott she said, "don't worry I will let you know how it goes with Scott ok Helen". I said, "Ok thanks Debs".

Later on she rang me to say he had done me proud and she also said, "The police would be sat outside the house over night just so that they knew we would be safe and ok", I said thank god, "thank you that's fine".

# *Monday 30ᵗʰ March 2009*

Monday morning, we all got up for the day to start children got ready for school then Richard and Cathy took the children to school.

I felt too ill to take them, plus I was too terrified to go out the front door. I locked myself in while Richard was gone.

My mobile phone rang, it was Liz Coles from CID, she says "Hi Helen, if it's ok with you we are coming round your house today about 11am, I'm brining my Sergeant with me Will White as he would like to discuss a few things with you. Is this ok with you Helen" I replied "yes".

Richard and Cathy came back from the school run and Cathy came in for a coffee Cathy said to me, "Helen you look terrible is their anything you need".

I said, "Yes please could you go and get me a new bra as"

"I just cannot face going out at the moment to buy one. I need one as they want me to go and have a medical and I need to have a new bra on", "Ok" she said, "I will go and get you one in a bit".

Cathy then said to me, "Whats going to happen now then".

"Have they finished with the house", I replied, "I really dont know" and at the moment I dont want to talk about it.

Cathy said, "Ok Helen I will go now and will see you later then".

"I will go and pick up a white bra from Marks a Spencers just ring me if their is anything else you want while Im out ok",

I replied, "Thanks Cathy I will see you later".

Liz and Debs came to the house at about 11.15am.

"Hi Helen how are you? this is Will White our sargent he is the main person dealing with this case" will white shook mine and Richards hand they came into the living room and sat down on the sofa, will said to me, "Helen I can't tell you how sorry I am for what this man has done to you".

I replied "thank you but you dont have to feel sorry".

I asked Will White if they had finished in the house he replied, "yes, we have for now but would it be ok Helen if we fitted the house with two cameras and put a security light on the back part of the house for extra security for you and your family"

I replied, "yes please if you dont mind as I feel terrified living here now".

"Ok Helen we will sort this out as soon as possible for you" he then asked if I was ok with having the panic button in the house he said, "do you feel a little bit safer knowing you have got that in place".

I replied, "not really I dont think I would be able to use it as I would freeze if anyone tried to break in again". He said, "Helen if you are worried about anything at any time you just press the button and the police response will be here in minutes I promise".

"Thank you will I wont use it unless I really think I have cause to but I now feel better knowing its here and you will be here fast as I am worried who Mark might know and they might try and get in". Will White then started to thank me for being very patient over the weekend.

He said, "It must have been very hard for you and the children".

"It was", I said as I dont have a large family that can help me.

I only have my mum who at the moment doesn't really know whats happening. I then asked, "Will, what is going to happen now".

"Well Helen Mark Shirley has offended before it was a long time ago", my facial expression must of changed at this point.

"Helen", he said, "I know this is going to be very hard for you but I have looked over your statement and because this case is so serious Im going to tell you that Mark is on a life lience for murder! Helen I can not give you any information as we need you to stay pure for the trial."

Well I just sat their and said, "please will you need to help me understand did Mark kill a lady please was her name Mary did Mark dis figure her face please I need these questions answered please I need to know".

"Im not really suppose to tell you but I have read your statement and yes her name was Mary Helen but I can't tell you anything else apart from we are trying to locate her family at the moment as what he has done to you is very serious and his lience conditions state that if he offened again the family are allowed to be contacted and told, Im really sorry but I can't tell you more as we have to protect you because if Marks defence thinks that you have been given any information on Marks past it would harm your evidence at the trial."

"The judge and the jury would prefer you to be as pure as possible" I felt very upset that no one could tell me the truth "I'm really sorry", said Will White "but it's for the best you need to trust us Helen" I agreed as much as I could, I did ask if they could let me know if and when they located Mary's family just for peace of mind.

Will White agreed he would we then sorted out with Liz when my medical was going to take place she said, "you can go to the bridge in the morning Helen if that's ok with you" but feeling very nervous I said to Liz, "can you tell me what the bridge is please as I've never heard of this place".

"Yes", she said, "it is a sexual health clinic, but upstairs in the clinic there is a piece of the building which they have called the bridge and it is just for victims of violent crimes and rape".

She said, "it's very private Helen and it's all locked in so you will feel safe ok, plus its women only there to treat you and look after you Richard can come with you do you want me to pick both of you up in the morning and take you".

"No, that's Ok Richard will bring me Liz if that's ok", Liz said that was fine but her and Debs would still meet us there, we agreed to meet there at 9.30am Will White then got up and said "Helen I will speak to you soon".

"Ok", I replied the rest of the day was so upsetting I just felt very upset and confused, they cant tell me much about Mary how can I tell them about the other angels, I'm so confused.

# Tuesday 31st March 2009

A very big struggle to get up today as there is a very big part of me, that doesn't want to face another day, trying hard for the children not to notice that mums not herself.

I told Richard that I didn't want to face going outside. "Dont worry", he said "I will take the kids to school they think its fun when I take them! So dont worry yourself."

I managed to get the children and the lunch boxes ready, I then gave them a big hug and kiss, told them I loved the and waived them good bye.

As the car drove away I got very upset, I cried (why why) has this happened to me while I sobbed to myself.

I just felt down in myself when Richard got back from school Cathy was with him they came in and Richard made a hot drink Cathy was trying to talk to me asking if things were ok, "whats going to happen now then Helen once they have done your medical"

I replied, "I really don't know Cathy" she then said, "I have your new bra here" and I said "thank you."

Cathy then said, "Helen do you want me to take you to the clinic today?"

"No thanks Cathy I want Richard with me by my side." I said.

"Ok dont worry Helen you know where I am if you need me." I replied, "Ok thanks Cathy".

Cathy left just after that.

I felt hurt when Cathy left as I couldn't help feeling and thinking she should be the one going through this not me he was not my partner.

I managed to have a very quick shower even though I felt so ill and very unsteady on my feet. I wondered if it was the diazipan tablets making me feel like this I thought I could hear Richard calling out to me, "are you ok it's nearly time to go to the clinic babe ok".

I said, "Nearly ready "my head then started to thump really bad and I felt dizzy and sick.

Try and calm down I was telling myself but this wasn't very easy to do.

I was panicking about going through the front door plus I was not sure about the clinic as I knew I would have to take my clothes off at the clinic so they could examine me I could feel myself panicking god they have to look at my body.

I can't do this Im to dirty and ashamed of the marks that he has left on my body.

I could hear Mark saying (they wont believe you if you tell). Richard shouted out, "babe we really need to go now or we will be late ok".

Traveling down to the clinic it was like I was in a daze. I could hear the radio and Richard talking but it sounded like it was a million miles away, all I could hear was Mark Shirley god it all seemed such a blurr the experience of this is very hard to explain.

When we arrived at the clinic we were met by a lady called Laura we were made very welcome we were then taken through the front doors and in to a lift we then went up to the top floor where Liz and Debs were waiting for us as promised.

We all went into a side room where they explained that Richard would be more comfortable. Then Liz was asked to take me to the examination room which was in the next room Richard said to me, "you will be ok babe Im waiting right here for you and not going any where ok".

I felt so hurt and ashamed walking through to the room, when I got inside the room the doctor said, "Helen try and relax" she then told Liz she would have to wait behind the screen while she examined me the doctor gave me a gown, "don't worry Helen take your time undress when you are ready theirs no rush take all the time you need."

"Ok thank you." I said, when I called the doctor to say I was ready she said, "Ok."

"Helen we need to take your DNA first is that alright with you"

I replied "Yes that's fine."

She came over to me and took a mouth swab first then she cut some of my hair then she cut all my nails short and scrapped the skin around my nails she then said, "Helen lay yourself down on the bed" and laying a full size blanket over my body.

Talking to me through out she managed to examine my private areas which hurt a great deal as I was bruised and sore, she managed to take all the swabs she needed for me it felt like time had stopped.

I then had to have a pregnancy test plus I had to have an aids test, they also gave me a test for Hepatitis B plus I was given some tablets for any infection he may have given me, even though you could not of asked for nicer people having all this done to my body I really did feel absolutely dirty and ashamed with myself the thought of what I had just had done to me made me feel violently sick and very sad I kept thinking why me.

I have been with Richard for all these years and neither of us has never looked at any other person and yet this man Mark Shirley has taken all this away from me!

When I got back to the room with Richard he said he had been ask for his DNA to be done as well plus he had met one of the councilors who told him how to expect things to be over the next few weeks, they also told him victim support would contact him shortly to offer him some support.

We said good-bye to them all and left the bridge when we got home I remember just sleeping, Richard woke me up to say, "Im going now to pick up the children ok babe".

I just nodded while Richard was gone.

I had a wash and went and changed my clothes when Richard and the children came in from school I could see the sadness in all their faces.

I did manage to cook dinner for them but with a struggle especially in the kitchen area the evening was very quiet later that evening. I put the children up to bed I couldn't help thinking how my children looked very sad and confused.

They really did not no what was happening around them the most they had been told at this time was that Mark had broken in to the house, I felt hurt my children should be happy this is just not fair to them Cathy's children are fine their not going through anything like my children.

I then started to feel very angry with Cathy the rest of the evening was silent Richard sat on the lap top and I just slept on the sofa this seemed for the best as I didnt know what to say to Richard, I think Richard felt the same as me its like Mark Shirley was sitting in the middle of us both.

# *Wednesday 1ˢᵗ April 2009*

Richard was put on leave from work for two weeks as he was not coping very well plus I was just a mess physically and mentally poor Richard was running the house a job he has never had to do before.

Because he was put on leave by CID, his boss wasn't happy he told Richard if he could not come back to work then he would have no choice but to sack him, Richard asked CID if they would contact him and explain the situation CID did speak to Richard's boss but again he was not very understanding my poor husband he just looked very sad, and confused he really didn't no what had happened to me on that day he looked very ill in the face but he was not giving in, it was written all over his face that he had to hold his family together what ever may be.

I felt so guilty for him it was like two people struggling to cope not knowing what to do around each other Liz and Debs from CID were trying hard to help us.

Over the next couple of days things just felt blurred. My older daughter Amy now knew the truth she really did look heart broken as for me her mother.

I could really see the hate she had for Cathy and Mark. Amy asked me if Cathy had told her children, I replied, "I dont know darling try not to blame Cathy."

"She did not know Mark was going to break into the house", Amy replied, "well why didn't he break in to Cathy's house?"

"I don't really know darling." She goes on and asks "Well why has he hurt you mum?".

"I dont know darling" I replied we just sat and cried together.

I was trying to comfort her best I could but she was very upset and confused.

The other two children knew there was more but they did not ask me, Liz my liason officer from CID kept on ringing me to see if we were all ok every time she rang me.

I would ask the same thing have you heard from Mary's family yet and I would get the same answer not yet Helen. Because we were not coping very well as a family I asked my mum if she would take the children away for the weekend she didn't look very happy about it but she did agree in the end, she took them on Friday 10th April for the weekend.

On the Saturday my children phoned to ask if we would travel down to Devon to see them as they were missing us I said, "Yes."

I would as I could hear that they were missing us but I did say that mummy could only stay for a little while they agreed.

God I panicked all the way to Devon I was so terrified of being out in the open, I managed to stay with them and my mother for about two hours I then told my children that we had to go home because mummy needed to sort out the animals. My little boy was so upset I was heart broken I felt so guilty for leaving them there.

By the time we got home I felt very ill, that evening Richard had to call an ambulance as I had a seizure, they wanted to take me to hospital but I was too scared to go.

Richard explained to the paramedics the pressure we were under. Sunday was a very long day without the children and my house was very much in my face. Mentally I felt wore out as I could not run from the crime scene or Mark Shirley.

The children came back from Devon, my mother said, "They had a goodtime but they did miss us both".

I was overwhelmed to have them back not having my children with me was like loosing my heart as we are never separated apart from school hours.

The next couple of days were very hard for both of us still trying very hard to keep everything to a normal routine for the children. Liz phoned on the 16th April to say, "Helen the cameras are ready to be fitted on the house was that ok"

I said, "Yes that was ok".

Liz replied, "We will come around shortly."

"Ok Liz but we need to do it before the children come home from school".

Richard dealt with the camera man I sat with Liz downstairs I asked if there was any news on Mary's family she said, "sorry not yet Helen"

Liz then said, "I have passed your details on to next link the lady. I have been talking to about your case is going to ring you to see if she can offer you and Richard some help,"

"That's fine Liz, thank you."

Once the camera man had fitted the cameras and came back downstairs Liz said, "Helen we will ring you to make sure all is ok, if you're worried about anything at anytime just ring me or Debs ok" and I said, "I will Liz thank you."

When Liz left I just sat in silence trying to think of away to try and tell Liz of the other angels, my head just felt so confused about what Mark had done upstairs in my house I didn't know how to explain to Liz or anyone I just felt like I was in a nightmare feeling so alone.

My mind was just full of Mary and Liz or Will White can't tell me anything to help me, I just want the pain to stop.

# Getting Through The Next Few Month's With My Family And C.I.D

Every day seemed to get harder Liz from C.I.D. rang me most days just to make sure I was ok.

Still no news on Mary's family!!

I wasn't taking the pace of home life very well the lady that Liz had said about contacted me, her name was Debbie she was an independent worker from next link.

She sounded very understanding on the phone, Debbie agreed to come to the house to help us sort out our social security as Richard had lost his job as C.I.D. had put him on leave and he really did not know what to do as he had never been in this situation before.

When she came she seemed very jolly in herself, right then Richard lets get stuck into any letter you might have and make some phone calls.

She helped Richard fill out his forms that we had collected from social security. She also made a few phone calls where Richard managed to sort out canceling the working tax credits.

Social security decided Richard could claim ESA but he would have to make sure he got regular sick notes from his G.P to send into them, for us to get paid every two weeks.

They allowed us as a family to have £102.00 every fortnight. We said to Debbie, "O my God how are we going to live on that, what about our bills and our mortgage."

Richard and Debbie applied for some form's to see if we could get some help with the mortgage.

Debbie Watts rang around a few companies to explain the situation; she was trying to see if they would put a few house bills on hold, including the mortgage company. To our shock and dismay most places were not very understanding.

Looking at Richard I could really see how worried he was. This is a man that had always worked hard to keep his family I thought.

I really felt like I'd let Richard down, I just really didn't know what to say to him.

Debbie tried to reassure us, "Dont worry you two, you both just need to stay strong, you both can stick together and beat this, you are not alone.

I will help you as much as I can! You are both too strong to let this man destroy you"

Richard agreed and smiled at me it was one of those looks where he was trying to tell me dont worry we will get through this together.

I felt sick to my stomache as I just felt this was all my fault, Mark Shirley was just all around me my house didn't feel like my home anymore I was terrified of indoors and outside.

I could still see him and smell him god I just felt so ashamed. Debs said, "trust me Helen you will get through this, you can ring me anytime you want to your not alone."

"Ok!, thanks Debbie" I said. When she left I felt so wore out emotionally.

I didn't really no what to say to Richard. Liz phoned later that day, "Helen how are you getting on with Debbie". I replied "Fine thank you."

"Did Debbie manage to help Richard sort things out", "yes she did thanks she is very good at her job I dont think Richard would of managed Liz if Debbie had not of helped us."

"Helen you should here from victim support this week is that ok"

I replied, "yes that's fine Liz", "I'm not on shift tonight Helen so if you need anything later just ring Debs my partner". "Ok Liz" I agreed.

The evening was terrible I hate this house I thought to myself it just seems to close in on me the darker it seems to get the more Im sat in the crime scene and the more I feel I want to die.

Over the next couple of days apart from Liz phoneing to check if everything was ok, and if their was anything I needed the tension in the house was terrible it was like me and Richard were so far apart Richard doesn't know whether he is doing right or wrong for me, Im really struggling around him.

The children are still going to school and they are doing ok at home, but its not as good as it normally is for them. I have managed to see my GP she is very understanding, I broke down in tears and told her, "I don't know what to do why has he done this to me and my family", "I don't know Helen", she replied.

We talked about Richard, "how is he coping Helen", Karen my GP asked.

"Not good or the children my daughter Amy is in pieces but Molly and Sam seem to be holding it together even though you can feel their hurting" I replied.

"Have you seen Cathy?" she asked.

"Yes a few times". Has she offered to help with the children? "No not really" I replied, but I wouldn't want her too as I like the children with us.

Cathy normally comes in for coffee after the school run with Richard, "how does that make you feel Helen", she asked "sometimes I feel I can't be bothered because I feel so bitter Im trying not to blame Cathy but its hard.

Part of me feels very embarrassed because it was her ex-fiance that's done this to me", I replied.

"I can fully understand", she replied "I just wish their was something more I could do for you Helen to help, what about your mum" she asked,

I explained that will white from CID had told my mum as much as he could as they have to keep me pure for court, "I feel my mum is so distant", I cried.

"The only one that shows she cares is my sister Mandy", we then spoke about Mary! I told her how I can't stop thinking about what Mark had told me, "CID can't give me any information apart from yes he did kill her", I cried.

My GP managed to calm me down, "Helen", she said "when are you seeing victim support", "later today" I said, "That's good make sure you come and see me in a couple of days unless you need me sooner", "Ok thanks for listening to me", I replied.

She gave me a hug and said "You are welcome you are not alone Helen."

She really made me feel like I had someone that cared I really needed to reach out to someone but as sad as it sounds it couldn't be my mother.

Later that day, I had a visit from Hanna from victim support she seemed very nice but it was very hard to talk to her. I just talked about the children; I also told her how all the neighbours weren't speaking because of all the rumours as they had seen lots of CID and police at my house,

"How long have you lived here Helen", Hanna asked.

I replied, "39 years on the estate but I have only lived in this house for 14 years,"

"That's a very long time" she said, "Have you ever had any trouble on this estate,"

"No never it's always been ok" I replied.

"It's such a shame you have had this trouble now." She said.

I told Hanna how scared I was about going outside she said, "Start with trying to take the children to school but just do it slowly Helen," "ok I will try" I said to her.

We made arrangements for Hanna to come in a week's time.

Over the next couple of days life was very much the same really Liz phoned a few times to cheek that everything was ok but still no news on Mary's family.

This was very hard for me as even though Mark Shirley had attacked me, all I could think about was 'Poor Mary'. I kept thinking about all the terrible things Mark had old me, 'Had Mark really defaced Mary!' My emotions and feelings were all over the place, I just couldn't justify why Mark had told me all these horrible tales. I'm not ever sure if they are true.

Why did he think I was Mary, why didn't Cathy even mention Mary!!

Strange I thought, Cathy popped round for coffee, "How are you coping is there any news on anything", "Not yet" I replied.

"Helen you dont look good you look very tired, have you had much to eat," she asked, "No not really" I said.

Cathy said, "Is their anything you want me to do,"

"Yes can you tell me about Mary?", I cried.

"Helen I feel so guilty if I could tell you I would but no I'm not allowed." She responded. "I am so sorry."

I could see in her face that she couldn't and I could see how hurt she felt but that didnt help me. When she left I felt very deeply hurt how can she watch a friend suffer like this I thought, she does know how we are struggling as a family.

Cathy text me a couple of hours later to say, "Helen I wish he had done this to me" she said she felt so sorry for what he had done "I feel so guilty Helen I wish I could take it all away from you but I can't."

I just sat and looked at the text message.

I decided for the sake of the children mine and Cathy's it wouldn't be fair to fall out over what Mark had done to me, but that didn't stop me feeling she must know more about him and his past so even though I felt very hurt and let down by someone that was supposed to of been my friend I didn't want to hurt the children it wouldn't be fair to them, so I text her to say, "Cathy its not your fault you dont have to feel guilty you didn't know Mark was going to do what he's done."

Cathy text me back to say, "thank you Helen Im glad it's not going to come between us but will always feel guilty,"

Cathy also said that she had a CID officer coming to see her to take a statement, "I will tell them as much as I can Helen to support you", I text back saying, "thanks Cathy."

As the day went on I managed to take my children to school with Richard God this was so hard, Liz kept phoning "is everything ok Helen, we will be out shortly to see you is that ok,"

"Yes that will be fine Liz", I asked Liz, "why Cathy was involved",

She said, "It's because she was with you from the start Helen plus because they needed as much information on what she knew about Mark."

I told Liz, "I had managed to leave the house to take the children to school."

"That's brilliant Helen well done." Liz asked, "How's things with Richard and you?"

"Not good", I said, "hes been so understanding Liz but Im just so terrified of everything Liz, I dont know what to do around him or the children and the house is really getting too much."

Liz said "Helen you just need to stay as strong as you can."

I told Liz what I had decided with Cathy for the sake of all the children, "thats good Helen as we need you to be strong around Cathy, as we need to get a lot of information from her about Mark for the court case." She said.

A few hours later, I sat thinking about what Liz had said I wonder what sort of information Cathy could give apart from what we already knew.

(Strange I thought) in away they are asking me to stay strong because they need Cathy's statement so that the court case will be stronger, this to me seemed very odd.

The following day I managed to do the school run with Richard we both spoke to Cathy at school, "why dont you come round and have a coffee later Helen" Cathy asked.

"I can't at the moment Cathy as Ive got to see the GP plus victim support are comming out to see me" I replied.

"Thats fine" she said, "maybe tonight then as Ive got the CID officer coming out to me anyway, plus Ive got to see the GP myself later."

"Ok, If I can manage it I will text you later to say I'm coming round."

As the day passed, I became more and more confused, when I spoke with the GP I told her how the passed couple of days had been and how Im struggling with every thing she highered my tablets as she didn't feel I was coping very well.

We spoke about my feelings towards Cathy she said, "Helen I do understand it must be very hard especially living next door to her", she told me that Cathy was seeing her later, she also told me how guilty Cathy felt, "Helen try and stay strong I will see you in a few days." "Ok, thanks" I said, she gave me a hug and said, "see you soon."

Later that, day victim support (Hanna) came to see me it was hard trying to talk to Hanna as I could hear my little boy having a tantrum in the other room because he wanted to be with me but we did manage to talk about how I was feeling we spoke together on how I felt about Cathy..

Hanna agreed with me it was odd that the GP and CID were both telling me to try and stay strong with Cathy because CID needed her as a strong witness.

I asked Hanna if we could change the time from 6.30pm in the evening to maybe daytime because of my children Hanna said she couldn't, we agreed same time next week.

That evening Cathy text me to say, "are you coming round for coffee?",

I did panic about it but Richard walked me round, once I had calmed down a bit inside myself it felt quite nice not to be sat in the crime scene.

Sitting in Cathy's house did sadden me as my children seemed low and yet Cathy's children seemed so happy.

Once Cathy settled them we started talking, she told me she had made a statement to CID Lisa Jones, Lisa would be dealing with Cathy, Lisa apparently would be in contact soon with me, she also told me that the GP had put her on leave from work for a few months.

She was also put on tablets, because she wasn't coping very well because of what had happened. She also said she would be getting victim support.

We spoke of Mark, it was like she was helping me to justify what Mark had done to me, but we could not talk about Mark's past as Cathy was told by Lisa we were not allowed because of the court case.

So even though I agreed to stay strong and friendly with Cathy, I'm sorry it was like she was convincing people she was a victim too.

She had all her family helping her with her children I just sat and listened to her feeling sorry for herself because she felt so guilty.

"Cathy," I said "I need to go home now."

"Ok Helen I will walk you round" she offered.

"Thank you" I said, "Helen you need to know I'm here if you need me" she tried to give me a hug, "see you in the morning bye."

When I went in my house I was so upset I told Richard he said, "Why is she acting like that, shes not the victim."

Richard seemed very angry we agreed it felt like we weren't being told much about Mark, what was going on what are they all hiding I just felt hurt. Richard stayed up for the night again to keep watch I managed to sleep alittle bit, again we just both had a bad night.

Over the next few weeks, it was about the same really CID would check that we were ok. Hanna from victim support would call to the house once a week. Richard had been given a victim support worker his name was Peter he was very nice Richard found Peter to be very understanding.

I would see Cathy in the evening time as she seemed to be sleeping her life away throughout the day apart from when Lisa CID had to see her or the GP she now had her victim support worker who called once a week in the morning.

Cathy said her worker was very nice I can tell her anything that's good I said, "I think your lucky Cathy to have one that can call when the kids are at school."

As for us as a family things seemed to be getting worse. I just seemed to be scrubbing myself away as I just dont seem to feel clean, still not sleeping very good. Richard looks pale and ill he still hadn't heard if they are going to help us with the mortgage.

On the 5th May 2009 my daughters Amy and Molly came in from school in a panic, whats wrong!

Mum we had a car follow us with three men inside, "where too?" I asked. Calm down girls. Just as we were walking through the bawa club car park which is at the top of our street it's a big field that the girls cut through on their way home from school.

I didn't know what to think, but they were scared, we managed to calm them, I spoke with Liz she said perhaps it was just someone driving through and the girls started to get scared.

The following day it happened again which really did panic me and Richard so I rang Liz she said, "Its very odd Helen you need to pick the girls up off the school bus as it is a worry because like you Helen we dont know who Mark might know, she was going to report it to Lisa and will the sergeant."

We managed to calm our daughters down and told them we would be picking them up from the bus stop, they agreed with this even though you could see in their faces they didnt want this embarrassment with their friends.

We also went into the school which we were advised to do by CID. School were very understanding they said they would make sure the girls were watched without their friends noticing just incase anyone was hanging around that shouldn't be.

We assured school we would keep them updated, myself throughout this felt very nervous I kept thinking god what if Mark has ask someone to hurt my girls.

Richard was watching the house incase and we made sure that the kids were picked up every day plus they had to stay in unless we knew where they were going.

Liz phoned to see if everything was ok, Liz also said, "Helen would you still like to see your statement," "Yes" I said, "ok me and Will can sort that out, is it ok if we come to yours in an hour, thats fine", I replied.

When they came I first asked will if there was any news on Mary's family! Not yet Helen you will be the first to know when we do, I decided with Will white that I didnt want to go through my statement I would wait untill we went to court as we didnt want the prosecution side to say I wasn't pure on the wittness stand.

Will White, said "He would be in touch soon", "Ok", I replied, Liz said she would call me. We all agreed this was for the best.

A couple of days later my youngest daughter Molly came down at about 11pm to say she had just seen a bald headed man in our back garden, she was very scared my dogs were barking. I didn't use the panic button Richard went out to look but he had gone! We reported it to CID.

They said to use the panic button if anything else happened over night, and they would come out to see us the following day. We managed to calm our daughter again my poor husband had to watch over night, as for myself God I was terrified inside didn't really know what to think. The following day it was decided by CID that they would put a letter out around the community to see if that might help.

THIS IS A COPY OF THE LETTER.

AVON AND SOMERSET CONSTABULARY

Our Ref: 00000000                                    Date: 13 MAY 2009
Your Ref: 00000000

Dear Sir/Madam,

**Reference: Suspicious Male seen in the Stanton Road and BAWA Club car park**

My name is Lisa Jones and I am a Detective working at Bristol CID. I am writing to you as well as several other neighbours in Stanton Road, Southmead in regards to a suspicious male that has been sighted in your area on Monday the 11th of May 2009.

This male is described as white with a bald head, he is described as being in his 30's and wearing dark clothing including a dark coloured hooded jumper.

This male has been spotted in the car park area of the BAWA club near Southmead Road between the times of 0700 to 0830 hours on that day. He was later spotted in the garden of a property on Stanton Road at around 11pm. This male was startled and ran off.

If you have seen a male similar to the description given above in your area on Monday the 11th of May 2009 at any time I would ask that you give me a call on the above number and pass on whatever details you may have. If you do not want to reveal your identity then please call Crime stoppers on 0800 555 111.

I would also ask that this male may simply be visiting someone in the area or may have recently moved in and if that is the explanation then again I would appreciate a call just to inform me of that.

Many thanks for taking the time to read this letter.


Yours Sincerely
Bristol CID

Over the next couple of days, I spoke with Liz to see if anything had come of the letter that was sent out she said no not yet Helen just try and stay strong Helen.

I kept thinking to myself god its easy for people to keep saying that but when you know your children are frightened and your husband looks really worn out it makes you feel so angry, I felt so guilty for them all.

The following day victim support Hanna called to see me Richard took the children to blaize castle a park nearby; my eldest son went with him Hanna and myself were talking about most things Hanna said about how worrying it must feel to have this man hanging around the garden and in the area.

I told her that a letter had gone out in hopes that someone might have seen something, just before Hanna left my phone rang it was Richard someone has stolen Scott's bike my heart just sank as he had worked hard to buy this bike, have you called the police Richard yes he replied! Hanna left saying Helen stay calm.

The police were very good they managed to find the bike but the youths that stole the bike had broken parts off it, Richard and Scott were told they would keep the bike to take prints from it my son was really upset, as for me I just felt I'd had enough.

Liz phoned me, she said they had spoken to Southmead road police station to waive the payment for storing the bike, I asked Liz if she felt that any of this was connected, she said she could not answer that, "I will ring you tomorrow Helen unless you need me before", "ok thanks Liz."

Over the next couple of days apart from hearing from Liz things were very much the same, Richard's looking very tired, my poor children really dont look good they are looking very tired as they are not sleeping very well, they are so scared of the house incase someone breaks in.

We are always telling them that things are alright but you can see in their little faces that they are frightened as they have never had any trouble in their home life before. I keep feeling so guilty for them. It was also very hard watching Cathy and her children this is so unfair I thought.

On the 14th May 2009 Lisa and Liz called to the house, "Hi Helen".

"Hi" I replied.

We all sat in the living room; I asked Lisa if there was any response from the letter that had been sent out about the bald headed man.

"No nothing", she said we spoke about a few things.

I also asked her if she felt if any of this was connected to the attack in March, we can't be sure Helen but we are doing everything we can.

Lisa said Helen if you feel that anything is happening in the garden or you think anyone is hanging around either use the panicbox or ring the police the house is on flag with the police station.

I told Lisa, that I didn't like to bother the police as I know how busy they are.

Lisa said, "Helen you are not a nuisance to us you never contact us so dont think that you have to sit here with no help that is what the police are here for and that is why we gave you the panic box".

"Ok", I replied. I will if I need help, again there was no news on Mary's family.

When they left myself and Richard, went to the local shops to get a few things.

Going to the shop panics me it made me feel so ill it made me feel dizzy sick and I felt like everyone was looking at me but as hard as it was I needed to keep trying because of my children and Richard.

When we got back from the shops Richard put the shopping away as for me I had to sit down and try and calm down.

After about hour I managed to put my dogs out in the garden, I asked Richard to make a hot drink I also noticed my son's guinea pigs were very noisey so I got their food out of the cupboard went round the side of the back garden to feed them and God I just stood looked at the cage.

"Richard!", I shouted, he came rushing out, God he said whats happened.

I don't know they were fine this morning someone had opened their small cage.

One guinea pig had a broken neck and they had just left him for dead as for the other one he was just screeching in his bed compartment.

I just stood and cried our little boy had bought them a few months ago with his grandmother's birthday money!

I think me and Richard just both felt sick to our stomach's, "Why Richard, why are they doing this", "I don't know babe", he just held me we both managed to put the other pig into a box we also put our rabbit in the box, I said to Richard, "we can't let these get hurt, not thinking straight", I said to Richard take me to the Lawrence Weston Farm.

We will ask them if they can take them as I can't let them get hurt, the person at the farm said they couldn't take them.

On the way home I just cried, Oh my God!!.

I thought these are my children's animals what am I trying to do I thought, I got very angry whoever is doing this to us will not get away with it, they won't win.

"Richard what are we going to tell the children", "I dont know", he replied.

When the children came home we had to tell them what had happened they all cried. My little boy with his dad went and buried the little guinea pig in the garden our son just sobbed.

I could hear Cathy's children playing God I felt so evil my son crying in his garden and yet Cathy's children are playing in their garden.

Our son nursed the other guinea pig with my help but the poor thing died of shock I felt so evil inside especially towards Cathy we reported it to CID who said their was nothing they could do.

Over the next few days life just got harder and harder. I felt so guilty my children looked so sad I really felt that Mark Shirley had the upper hand all the time their still wasn't any news on poor Mary's family so again I just had to try and cope around my family.

I didn't want to show them how I was crumbling deep down inside, my eldest son Scott came home from his Nan's house.

"Mum", he said "Mark has a girlfriend and she lives the other side of the estate her name is Tanya",

"Scott why are you telling me this? Im really not interested darling",

"Mum she has a bad house" Scott said.,

"What do you mean Scott?", I replied.

"She has youth taking drugs in there".

"Scott I really don't want to know mum", he said.

"She has put ten pounds on my head unless I tell CID that I didn't see Mark Shirley at our house on the 20th March the day you were attacked mum", straight away.

I started to panic, "Mum its ok, Im not frightened of them".

"Scott don't be silly we need to keep you safe darling." I responded.

I tried to talk my son into not being the main witness as I didnt want him hurt, but know he wouldn't agree with me we decided to ring Liz from CID her partner Debs came out and took a statement from Scott about what Tanya had threatened.

CID also sent the police security Bobby van to my mother's house to secure her house as Scott stays there's a lot plus they flagged my mother's house with the police station.

They did take Tanya to court she was given a fine for witness intimidation.

I can't express how hard the next few weeks were. I was so terrified they were going to hurt my son, my son just stayed very strong, mum he kept saying they can keep stealing and damaging my motor bikes they can beat me up if they want but nothing is going to stop me going to court for Mark Shirley for what he's done to you mum.

I felt so proud of my son but very worried for his safety, mum I also need to tell you that Tanya has a son he's slowly mixing his way into a crowd of youths thats been hanging around on the far corner by our house.

"Ok", I replied, "Dont worry the youths round here have never bothered us before Scott.

I know they play the neighbours up but not us just make sure dad keeps an eye on them." I could really see how worried my son was really.

The following day, I couldn't find my old cat I was really worried for her. As she didn't normally go far a few hours later my neighbour knocked my door he told Richard that our cat was on a big stone in his pond.

Richard went down his house he brought baby the cat home she was still alive but in a very bad way.

We rushed her to the vet; the vet had to put my cat to sleep as she had to many injurys the vet said.

"She had been kicked and beaten", I just cried.

I really felt I didn't want to live anymore, my poor animal's why would anyone want to hurt my animals they are so innocent; again the police couldn't comment or do anything.

As for my children, they were devastated especially my daughter Amy as she had baby the cat for ten years. I felt so sad for her I just didn't no what to say to her we have always been very close but I was just lost for words.

That evening when the others were sleeping I sat with my daughter Amy we both talked and cried she held on to me so tight again asking why is this happening to us mum, she was trying to be so grown up at the age of thirteen bless her it was alot for her to go through.

She told me how much she hated Cathy and Mark I managed to settle her eventually, when she was asleep I just sat and looked at her.

I felt so hurt and sad. She is right I thought why has this happened to me and my family I could really see why my husband and children disliked Cathy I could also see why they resented Cathy, as her children like my children only met Mark a handfull of times and yet he's done what he's done to me and my family.

Yet Cathy and her children are living life to the fullest; shopping trips, outings and a two week holiday.

My poor family, I thought. We are struggling on £102 per fortnight not knowing where the next meal was coming from all our savings had gone everything is such a mess. My children use to have everything they never went without but now we have hardly anything to live on.

All my husband's hard work wasted, bless him. He looks so worn out there is nothing I can do. I feel Im trapped in a dirty bubble just waiting for the next thing to happen, I feel so guilty I never thought something like this would of happened to us.

Over the next couple of days, things were very much the same really, we did notice Tanya's son in the crowd of youths we also noticed that the youths were starting to play football outside our house.

We didn't take any notice my children couldn't go out to play because of the comments "Your mums saying she was raped!", plus they would say, I was a dirty tramp, we just ignored them. My childrens bikes got broken in our back garden, When we were out. Again the police took the bikes for finger prints but there was nothing they could do. I think for me and my family life was getting worse.

I asked CID if they could move us out of our house, to be told no because we were private owners not council tenants. This seemed very unfair for my children who were terrified.

They were starting to look very tired and ill I had no friends or family to help, so we just had to try and make things as good as we could for the children.

Richard's mother lives in Germany but she never offered to have her grandchildren or myself over to Germany to give us all a break.

She said she was to busy and going on holiday to the states in America, not knowing what to do we just hung on to one another and carried on with each horrendus day!

Not knowing what to expect next. I would still have Debbie from next link who was very good to me she would visit or chat on the phone. Hanna from victim support I couldn't see weekly as I found it to much with the children, I didn't think it was fair to them and Liz would phone most days to see how things were going.

Karen my GP was brilliant you wouldnt meet a nicer person she treated me like a friend not just a patient, Richard had Peter from victim support again he was a very nice person.

I think Richard felt he could talk to Peter about anything and take as long as he wanted Peter would just sit down in our house like a friend.

We noticed that the youths were moving away abit they were slowly going back across the road and sitting on the green box on the corner of our road.

They were still playing most of the neighbours up the only time they bothered us was if we opened our front door they would shout abuse across the road, apart from our kids not going outside and still being terrified of them we just ignored them.

The neighbours would call the police for the noise and the drinking but we didn't get involved we stayed in and Richard would just be on lookout in case they did anything to our cars or our house.

# On Saturday 6<sup>th</sup> June 2009

My husband took our youngest son Sam and eldest daughter Amy to the shops it was around about 7.30pm Richard kept ringing to see if me and my other daughter were ok.

Richard asked, if he could get the children a treat (Mcdonald's) we couldn't really afford it but he didn't want to tell them now.

The Children agreed to have happy meals, which was a blessing as its only six pounds.

While they were gone we sat with the TV on, my daughter Molly said, "Mum I dont want to scare you but there is a man watching us through the consevatory window".

I looked through my open plan room and God I froze, he was just looking at us "mum" mum what shall we do",

I couldn't even tell my daughter to ring the police or press the panic button as I honestly just froze to the seat. My twelve year old daughter Molly had the sense to press the panic button!!

The police arrived they gave chase but didn't catch him. They were very good, they responded very quickly.

As for my daughter they were both very brave, I was just terrified. Afterwards, I felt so ashamed a parent is supposed to protect their children not just freeze I felt useless.

My husband Richard said Helen it's not your fault you have been through too much, Richard looked so guilty for going to the shops bless him, I also felt so bad because we used the protection button.

The police praised my daughter Molly which was nice. Once everything had calmed down, I settled the children and then went in the bath to scrub my body. God only knows what my body must look like. It felt so sore where I kept scrubbing but I still couldn't bring myself to look down, I hadn't looked at myself since Mark attacked me but I've got to keep scrubbing as I feel so dirty and angry with myself and Mark Shirley.

The following day I felt shook up, Liz phoned, "Helen are you ok?", "yes", I replied

"Liz I suppose there is still no news on Marys family", "Not yet but will white is still working on it." Liz said.

"Do you need me to come out to you next week, Helen?", "I dont mind Liz its up to you", "we do need to talk about a few things Helen", "ok that's fine Liz".

Liz said she would ring me to confirm a day and a time, that evening Cathy text to ask if I was going round for coffee. The children were settled; Richard walked me around to Cathy's house. it was nice just to be out of the crime scene.

Cathy's children were very bouncey! Full of jokes, part of me just felt sick and hurt but I couldn't just get up and go home as that would have seemed rude.

But I kept thinking about how my children were before all this happened, family life was so full before all this yet it's now felt so empty.

Once Cathy had settled her children she started chatting about the children, what she had bought them and family life in general, she started telling me how good her family have been to her through this hard time, she said her victim support worker was very good.

I felt that she was sensing that I really wasn't interested which at this time I wasn't. I felt quite hurt inside as apart from Richard standing by me, my own family ie: my mother and my closest sister they hadn't supported me from the start of all this, I looked at Cathy and thought how lucky you are.

A big part of me felt so angry as she hasn't lost anything from being Marks partner, but my life and family have been destroyed.

She went on to the subject of Mark how she loved him, this was very hard for me I remember saying Cathy I know how much you loved Mark but I can't justify with you why he's done this to me, she did say how sorry and guilty she felt, again I told her I didn't blame her.

Cathy said that's because you don't know everything yet Helen, Cathy what do you mean!!!

I've done something bad on the parole board meeting, what do you mean Cathy!!!

I told some lies but I can't tell you because of court, Im so sorry Helen.

I really didn't no what to think mainly because my brain didn't think very straight what with the way my life was, plus all the medication I was taking at this time, but Cathy did say if she had of none this was going to happen she never would of told lies at the parole board.

Cathy, I don't know what the lies are but it can't be that bad surely!

That is how both of us left the conversation, when I went home I told Richard neither of us knew what to think. Deep down inside of me, I very much felt Cathy knew alot more which made me feel that she knew Mark was dangerous, which hurt me alot as she is my friend we have always tried to help her where we could as a family plus the children were all so close.

On Monday 8th June 2009 we went shopping with the children it was early evening, when we got back to our house their were two rough looking men banging our front door, my children looked very scared.

I told Richard who was just about to get out of the car to wait, as they started to walk down the garden path looking very angry one of them started shouting and banging the car window. Tanya's son and a few others were their on our garden wall, my children started screaming I looked at my family, I got very angry!

Shaking I got out of the car walked round to Richard's side pushed the man out of the way, stood by Richard's door and asked the man if he had a problem as he was scaring my children, he replied Im going to kill your bloke, he went to push me out of the way! I told him if he put one finger near me he would be in trouble with the police, he said call them I'm not bothered.

I shouted to my daughter Amy ring the police he then got very abusive in his manner, he started saying that the youth's had told him that my husband had put his little boy in the boot of our car and scared him so that is why he was coming down to our house to sort my husband out.

I just looked at him and said if you heard this through Tanya's son who is stood right their and if you live by Tanya who has also told you then Im sure the police will sort it all out when they get here but I can assure you my husband hasn't done anything as he doesn't go out he's to busy looking after his family because I've been attacked.

He started to get angry just as the police arrived I managed to call Cathy who was watching through her window not that she helped me before the police came.

I managed to get my children from the car they went in Cathy's house terrified. The police sorted the two men they really stripped them down.

Tanya's son was also stripped down they made them all leave the street, they were firmly told to stay away from our address.

My poor husband was so angry and upset with me, I think he was so scared for me because I confronted them, but I didn't want him hurt for something he had not done he would never hurt a child.

I really dont know where I managed to stand up for my family, the anger just came over me, my children they were crying they looked so scared I just thought enough is enough. I was so exhausted when we settled the children that evening, I also felt so shocked and scared inside, but at least I managed to protect my family.

The following few days were hard especially with the children who looked like they were all just waiting for the next thing to happen, its very hard when your trying to keep everything as normal as possible for the children on a day to day.

When so many things keep happening, we have had very little money coming in the household, so we can't even treat the children to anything nice.

I feel so upset and sad for them the only release for them at the moment is school. Even though they have been brilliant throughout!

They keep saying mum can we go to the shopping mall or bowling. I would have to say no sorry I have no money at the moment. A few times they would look at me and say but mum Cathy's children are still doing every thing, or they would say but we want to meet our friend's from school.

I would just sit in another room by myself and cry I would feel so guilty, if only I hade of done more on the day of the attack I thought, why didn't I do more, deep down inside I just wished Mark Shirley had of killed me.

Over the next few weeks, I managed to work with Liz on the video footage of what happened on the day of the attack for court.

I found this to be very hard, it was very disturbing trying to explain what Mark had done to me on my kitchen table, I thought making the statement was hard but when you have to be interviewed under camera its alot harder as alot of your inner feelings do come out.

Liz was very understanding she made me feel like I had plenty of time if I wanted to take a break I could.

Even though she was a CID worker she always put her wholeself forward like a friend. She always made me feel like I wasn't just another victim, plus Richard was still being very understanding, he would take me to the interviews.

Richard tried to support me best he could. He would sit in a side room just waiting for me to come out.

I would feel very guilty after doing the video footage for my family as I would just go into some sort of shell as the day went on, as I found the footage really hard trying to explain the attack it was very hard because it's like your re-living the pain of whats happened.

But even though it's hard, you keep telling yourself your doing good because its for the judge and jury to get a better picture of what this offender has done. Plus, I thought it would help in the courtroom when the defence has got to ask me questions.

The only problem I had with these interviews was that I felt I was letting myself down and other's because I couldn't bring myself to tell what Mark Shirley had done upstairs in my house to me.

There are too many angels I kept thinking they can't tell me what he's really done to Mary and they haven't asked me about anyone else so how can I tell them there are more angels.

My mind kept thinking perhaps Mark Shirley has just tried to scare me more, but why would he dress me and treat me like others.

I feel so confused about what Mark Shirley has done. I didn't know who to tell my mind is feeling wore out as I'm trying to put all these angels in some sort of order in silence, I need to tell

Cathy was good support in the evenings after these interviews. I think Cathy knew how hard it was for me.

She would just say, "did it go ok?".

"I would just say yes! I'm fine."

Then we would have a coffee, she would just talk about other things, she would always's say Helen later if you can't sleep or if your paceing around just text it doesn't matter what time, the thought was nice, but apart from sitting in Cathy's house most evenings.

I never disturbed her overnight. As time went on Lisa from CID rang and gave me a date for the palimary hearing at Bristol Magistrates Court for Mark Shirley.

The date of the hearing was the 30th July 2009; Lisa gave me a list of what Mark Shirley was being charged with, those being six charges of

FALSE IMPRISONMENT, COMMITTING AN OFFENCE WITH
INTENT TO COMMIT A SEXUAL OFFENCE, RAPE AND THREE
CHARGES OF ASSAULT BY PENETRATION.

We were told very firmly that we weren't allowed to attend the court, plus we weren't allowed to discuss it with anyone, I asked Lisa if I needed to get a solicitor as I felt we weren't being told much, Lisa said we normally tell victims no as we use our own legal barristers, she said you will have a barrister at court Helen.

I asked Lisa if I would meet with the barrister before the hearing.

She said normally Helen victim's don't but she would see what she could do, we ended the conversation with Liz or Debs will ring you to let you no the outcome of the hearing Helen, as we should get a Crown Court date for a full hearing.

At this stage I felt so confused it just makes you feel that even thou you are the victim you dont have any say in anything, they seem to just update you and tell you what your allowed and what your not allowed to do.

Richard couldn't understand why we weren't allowed to be part of the palimary hearing I think he felt that he wanted to be there.

We just both wanted to know what was going to happen, plus we felt it was our right to no what was being said about the attack.

We rang a few solicitors in Bristol to be told that rape cases are normally dealt with through CID and CPS they have their own barristers to deal with these type of cases, so we both felt we just needed to sit tight and just work with CID like we have done so far how ever hard it gets, we just had to have faith in them.

Every day just got harder and harder just waiting for the date for the Crown Court hearing!

The youth's were still sitting across the street, my children were still on their guard you could still see how they were just waiting for more things to happen.

Richard was still seeing Peter from victim support. Plus, he was still not sleeping at night as he kept watch over the house so the children could feel safe.

As for me I was just not copeing, apart from all the washing myself as I just didn't feel clean, it just felt like Mark Shirley had control all the time, sometimes I would just feel confused about who I was ie: Helen or Mary.

One evening, when I was sat in Cathy's having a coffee I received a text from Liz it was 10.20pm it read, "Hi Helen can I call you I have news from Wales", my heart just sank,

Cathy said, "What's wrong Helen?", Nothing Richard needs me so I have to go home".

"Do you want me to walk you round", "No its ok it's only next door." I responded.

When I got in I said Richard, "Liz has text she said she has news from Wales." Richard said, "You need to stay calm are you ready for her to ring you,"

I know my head and heart felt like they were exploding.

Liz phoned, "Hi Helen are you ok, "yes" I replied.

"Helen we have found Mary's family! Helen are you still there?", "yes Liz Im here,"

"Did you hear what I said we have found Mary's family!"

"Yes I heard you Liz are they ok Liz,"

"I think so", she replied.

"I wanted to be the first one to tell you Helen!.

"Thanks Liz, what happen's now?" I asked.

"Helen, I don't know I haven't been told. Will White will update me tomorrow but I just wanted you to know they have been found."

"Liz do they know what Mark has done,"

"Helen, I can't tell you anything tonight, as soon as I know more I will ring you,"

"Ok thank's Liz." I said.

When I came of the phone, Richard held me I really just didn't know what to think or feel, my emotions were all in pieces, I just felt that I needed to reach out to someone that knew Mary!

God it was just another very long night.

The following morning, I managed to take the children to school with Richard. When we got back from the school run, we cleaned the house together.

Richard said, "Why don't you ring Liz?"

"No I dont like to I will wait for her to ring me."

Every hour felt like two, then around about mid-morning Liz rang she said, "Helen is it ok if myself and Will White come out to see you today?,"

"Yes that's fine are you both coming out to me because of Mary's family,"

"Helen", she said, "Will White needs to talk to you himself, see you soon," "Ok Liz thanks", I really didn't know what to think.

When Will White and Liz came, Will said "how are you feeling Helen about us locating Mary's family".

I said, "I dont really know Will. There's a very big part of me that feel's sad for them having to face this after all these years. But the other part of me feel's, like it just want's to reach out to them because of Mary!

I dont know Will, I have mixed feelings about it I dont even no the truth."

"What do you mean Helen?", Will said.

"What I mean is I dont know whether Mark has done what he said to Mary or not.", "you can't tell me the truth."

Cathy next door can't tell me anything even though I know she's hiding alot of history on Mark, so all I've got to hold on to is what Mark told me on the day he attacked me thinking I was Mary!

I dont know what to think or feel, everything is such a mess. Will White went on to say Helen you have been brilliant you have stayed strong you have helped us with everything we have needed.

So I'm going to tell you, "yes Mark Shirley did kill Mary Wainwright, but we can't give you detail's of the murder as we need to keep you pure for Crown Court!".

I just looked at Will White and I felt numb "ok thank you for telling me Will.

He went on to say that they have spoken to Mary's family, they have explained Mark had re-offended.

They hadn't given them too much information. He also said that CID had decided it wouldn't be good for me or them to meet at this point because of court as CID needed me to stay strong and pure.

Plus if we were to meet, Mark's defence could say anything in court which could damage the case.

I fully understood what Will was telling me as much as I felt heart broken I just felt I needed to reach out to someone that knew Mary!

I agreed with Will that I would just continue to work along side Liz and stay as strong as I could for the sake of the court hearing.

Will White thanked me. He said, "Helen you and Richard have been very understanding you have been so strong, thank you."

He said, "Liz would be updating me with the court date," "ok thanks Will", I replied.

When they left I felt really let down I understood what Will White had said but I had waited a long time for them to find Mary's family in hope of learning the truth so again I just felt like Ive been left with a big empty hole deep inside me.

A few days later Deb phoned me from CID, Hi Helen we have a date for Crown Court its going to be the 4th November 2009, Liz will update you more on Monday, "ok thanks Deb", I said.

I just sat for a while before telling Richard because inside myself I was really panicking!

Oh My God! I have to sort the children out before the trial, I also started feeling very worried (God) Mark Shirley will be in the court room what if Im not strong enough to do this, what about Mary's family!

My inner feelings were really shaken. When the children were settled in bed I told Richard.

He said, "Its good, at least we have a date.

"Dont worry we can get through this together, I love you," he said.

"Im not going anywhere not now or in the future we will get through this together."

I felt a warmth inside, hes been through so much over the last few month's hes so pale, but I could see in his pale face and tired eye's how much he does love me and the children. My emotions were very mixed I love my husband so much, but deep down inside I felt so ashamed because of what Mark Shirley had done.

Over the weekend, we had a few problems with Tanya's son and youth's, my children were all settled in their beds when the youth's decided to target our house with abuse and threats they were trying to smash our windows.

Our children were scared; I put them all in the back bedroom I told them to stay there. I pressed the panic button for the first time as I didnt want my husband to go out and confront the youth's.

The police were at my house within minutes, the youths were warned to stay away.

No arrests were made, just verbal warnings. All over the weekend my children stayed in one bedroom at night because they were scared. I stayed with them, Richard just watched over the house my poor family they looked so pale and tired, I kept thinking God what is going to happen next, I felt so guilty.

I kept thinking what if I drop the charges on Mark Shirley would all the threats and trouble stop, or would Mark just come back out and kill me or my daughters.

It really felt like I was to blame. I hated myself for what my family was going through it was like being tortured in a nightmare where you just don't know where to run.

On Monday Liz phoned me, "Hi Helen I heard about the weekend how are you all?"

I explained to Liz what had happened, "The children must of been really scared Helen,"

"Yes" I replied.

"Im really pleased you managed to use the panic button Helen,"

"Yes I had no choice Liz, I didnt want Richard to confront them plus I wasn't sure if they were going to break the windows.

The police were very good Liz they came in minutes they didnt make any arrests but they did warn the youths to stay away."

"That's really good Helen, hopefully they will leave you all alone now,"

"Im hoping so Liz", I replied.

"Helen Debs gave you the trial date, how do you feel about it,"

"I'm feeling very scared Liz. How many days do you think trial will be for?" I asked.

Liz replied "Helen I think it's for about a week. It could be a little longer it depends plus the barrister that CPS has got on your behalf is Rosie Collins. She is very nice, Helen. She got lots of experience in rape cases.

"I have been told that you are allowed to meet with her shortly but because in most cases CPS don't allow victims to meet with their barrister.

Prior to court Rosie Collins won't be allowed to discuss the trial with you, as you have to stay pure because of the defence.

"What do you mean Liz", I asked, "well it can't be seen as Rosie Collins is leading you to say things that might not be right because Mark's defence can make Mark's side of the case look alot stronger, as the judge and jury prefer the victim pure." I could see what Liz was trying to say.

The following day, I went to see Karen my GP as I wasnt feeling well. I had a long talk with her; we spoke about how my counciling was going at the bridge.

I told her how I was really struggling with my counselling, why are you struggling Helen are you finding it hard talking about the attack.

I sat in Karen's room in tears. Im not allowed to talk to my councilor about the attack that is why I'm struggling.

Why aren't you allowed Helen, because my councilor has been told by CID that I have to stay pure for court, what do you 'mean' counselling is private, its supposed to help people through difficult times Helen.

That's what I thought, but Im only allowed to talk about everyday things, plus Im really struggling with the traveling down there because I really panic going out, so by the time I get to the bridge Im really puffed out emotionally.

Helen the way your being treated is terrible, Karen my GP then asked me how things were with Hanna from victim's support, again I told her how I was struggling as Hanna can't call to me in the day time, its very stressfull in the evenings because of the children.

Karen my GP then said so really you're not having much help or support apart from when you come up to my surgery to see me.

I just cried, Karen I really don't want to be here anymore, I wish in my heart that he had of just killed me!

Karen my GP just held me and said Helen I wish I could do more to help, Karen I replied you are the only one that I can turn to you have helped me right from the start.

Helen, what about your mum how are things with her. Have you managed to get support from her, not really Karen apart from Will White giving mum a small outline of the attack my mum don't never ask and I never lean on her.

"Why Helen?" Because she's making me feel like I've let her down. "What do you mean Helen you haven't let anyone down especially your mum."

Whats happened is not your fault. But Karen, that's how my mum makes me feel when I see her. We have always been close. Plus, out of all my mum's children, I'm the one that has always been there for her. Now, I feel that my mum's making me feel like I've let my sister down. "Why Helen?" because when CID first came to my house in March just days after the attack

I was supposed to have gone out for the evening with my sister for her husband's birthday. I thought my mum was dealing with telling them. But I don't think my mum has

But I could not make the evening out because I'd been attacked. Karen my GP said "surely Helen your sister would understand. Has she called to see you or phoned you?"

I cried, she's always been not only a sister but a very close friend we have always shared everything.

I'm feeling so lost and lonely without her I've always loved her to bits. But I haven't heard from her. The only time I get to hear how she is when my mum mentions her. Im sad because shes making her final plans to move to abroad. What if I don't get the chance to see her before she goes?

Helen Im sure if you ring her or write her a letter things will sort itself out. I can't Karen I don't want to offend my mum, maybe things will be more sorted around the trial Helen.

"I'm sure your sister will want to be there to support you", she said. Karen gave me a hug and told me to come to see her at the surgery when ever I needed to, even if it was just to talk.

"I'm here for you Helen" comforting words from Karen my GP.

"Thank you, Karen" I responded.

Over the next few weeks, things were about the same I did have a long talk with Hanna we both agreed that she wasnt the right worker for me as.

She could not do days and my little boy was to upset when she called in the evening. Richard was still seeing Peter from victim support every week, Peter was very nice.

He would come in to my home like a family friend, victim support did offer me another worker but I just didnt feel I could start again with a new worker, but I did very slowly start talking to Peter with Richard, plus Liz would phone me most days.

As for the bridge the two sessions a week just got harder, we would just talk about the children or we would talk about the finances and how we were struggling.

Over the next few weeks, even though things were still very hard, we met with Rosie Collins the barrister. She just explained to me what sort of things to expect in court. She asked me if I wanted a screen in the court room so Mark could not see me. But, I replied "No, thank you."

When we came away from the meeting Lisa and Liz walked up the road with us to our car.

Lisa Jones said, "Helen we have had a small meeting and we have decided that we are going to take the panic box away from your house,"

I replied "why?"

Lisa replied, "We don't want you to mistake youths in the area against proper criminals,"

I replied, "I've only used it once on the youths and that was because they were all trying to break my windows and myself and my children were scared," she replied, "we will collect it tomorrow".

I just said, "Ok", God inside I was now feeling very alone and terrified. Richard didn't really know what to think.

Over the following weeks it was alot of stress for me and Richard, we had to sort the children out ready for the trial.

My sister Mandy agreed that she would take them to brean for a week or so, I felt ever so gratefull to her as I had no one else to ask.

Money was a very big problem as we didnt have any, I went down to my Aunties house to ask her if she could help me, but no she didn't help, I ended up asking my dad for help, dad just sat and cried he said he wanted to go to court with me but I didnt want to put him through that.

Dad helped me pay for the caravan and food plus he lent me money for the children to have spending money.

About a week later it was time to take my children to brean. I've not had much seperate time from my children unless they have been at school, the emotions of leaving them at brean was not nice they cryed and so did I, the pain of this was terrible.

They looked so sad my sister Mandy rang me that evening to say don't worry the children will be fine with me. It was very sad without them I just felt lost.

# THE COURT PROCEEDINGS

On Wednesday 4th November 2009 my barrister Rosie Collins opened the court case at Bristol Crown Court; the case was to be heard by his honorable judge.

I had been told by CID that I wasn't needed in court untill Thursday 5th November 2009, as Rosie Collins had to put full history of Mark's previous offence(murder of Mary Wainwright) plus she had to give the history of the charges of the offence's of which Mark Shirley had done to me.

I was very upset and terrified for most of the day, the fault of them at court really made me feel ill, I was dreeding going to court in the morning, Karen my GP gave me some diazipan tablets to try and keep me calm, over night I didn't get much sleep I was to nervous.

Morning came very quick, myself and Richard got ready for court.

Richard was trying his best to support me.

Both dressed in our suits we left the house for court. When we got to the court Liz and Debs were waiting for us they took us straight to the witness area, where we met the wittness workers, they were very nice they made us a drink and showed us where to sit.

Liz and Debs were trying hard to talk to me but to be honest even to today I can't really remember what they were saying. At 10.30am I was called to go up to court room one.

Liz my Liaison officer and the wittness support worker took me up, god I was so terrified it was like my legs were made of stone, when we got to the court door Liz said, "you will be fine just stay calm, if you need to take a break at anytime just ask Helen."

The wittness support lady took me through two big doors to the court room.

Walking through I had the judge sat at the front top part of the court room, at the back of the court behind a glass screen I had Mark Shirley, across from the witness box

I had the jury, and Rosie Collins and Mark Shirley's defense were just to the side of the wittness box sort of in the middle of the court room, then their were seats for the public it was terrifying.

I got into the the wittness box and took my oath it felt like Mark Shirley's eyes were burning through the side of me, but I knew not to look at him I just looked at Rosie Collins and the jury.

The judge was very nice he told me to sit down, he also told me if at anytime you need to take a break Mrs Stockford please just ask, "Thank you", I replied.

Rosie Collins started to talk, she told the court how I was home alone on 20th March 2009 when Mark Shirley broke into my house, Rosie Collins ask me to explain what happened on the 20th March 2009, when I found Mark Shirley at my kitchen table I managed to explain to the court how I had been cleaning upstairs, when I came down Mark was sat at my table.

I explained how I asked Mark what he was doing in my house, I also asked Mark to leave. He said, "He had come for coffee."

I asked him again how did you get in. Again, Mark didn't answer.

I told them. Rosie Collins then asked me to explain how he looked on the day, I managed to describe him as being pale and he didn't look himself, what happened next Helen, Rosie asked!

I managed to tell Rosie Collins and the court how Mark said I was a nice lady and I needed to trust him, he told me to sit down on one of my kitchen chair's which I did as I didn't like the look on his face and felt scared, what happened then Helen.

He made himself a coffee, still telling me that I was a nice lady and I needed to trust him, Mark then went on to say that he once new a lady, her name was Mary!

Then what happened Rosie asked, Mark came across to where I was sat and stood in front of the chair, he was telling me as he was leaning over the chair with me sat on it, that Mary was a very trustful lady, I asked Mark to stop as I didn't know anyone called Mary!

"He then got angry", then what Helen Rosie asked, "he started telling me how he had watched Mary for a long time through her washing line's.

He started telling me that Mary smelt sweet," then what Rosie asked me, I started to tell the court how he started to remove my clothes, as he wanted me to trust him and he wanted to make me smell as sweet as Mary.

He pulled out a knife from his waist band, how did that make you feel Helen can you explain it to the court, it made me feel very scared the look on his face and in his eye's I knew to do anything that he wanted me to do.

He started to tell me that he had broke into Mary's flat.

He made Mary sit on a chair while he destroyed her home, he told me how he dragged her around.

He started arguing with himself, he was having a tantrum it was like he was talking to Mary, how did that make you feel Helen, I was very scared didn't really know what to do as I was terrified to move.

But he wasn't talking to me it was Mary that he was arguing with, what do you mean Helen can you explain to the court.

I firmly believe that he was talking and treating my body like Mary. He started to rape me. But, all the way through it Mark used my body but with Mary's name.

"How did he rape you, Helen?" Rosie asked. I managed with tears to ask for a break!

I got outside the doors with the usher, as the door closed behind me, I said to the usher Im ready to go back in, she looked at me and said we just this minute come out, "I no", I replied, it was like something was with me pushing me with force to go back in, I felt really strange.

I went back into the witness box and the judge asked if I was ok as I hadn't taken a break, he said, "Are you ok to carry on Mrs Stockford,"

"Yes", I replied.

Rosie asked me to explain the rape and how it made me feel, I managed to do this, it felt like I had someone sat with me telling me and pushing me to tell everything, the strength felt very strange.

I also managed to tell the court on how he had raped and killed Mary.

I also managed to tell them how he had left a 2p on Mary's body and a knife.

I managed to tell them how he had wrapped her in cloth, how he was laughing at Mary's last breath.

"What happened next Helen", Rosie asked, he was having a tantrum because he hadn't brought a 2p or a knife to put on Mary.

I think he ment me, eventually court ended for the day, it was a very hard day, I felt so ill. Liz and Deb's both said, "well done".

I had to be back in court for 10am Friday morning to go back on the stand.

When we got back home in the evening from the court, the house was so empty with the children not there, I was missing them so much, I did speak to them by phone but they sounded so sad, my little boy was so tearful. I didn't see my mum she didn't come round, Cathy text me to say, "how was it today Helen,"

I text back saying, "we can't talk because we are not allowed but it was a very hard day!" The mood between me and Richard was very quiet.

Friday 6th November 2009, Liz and Deb's met us both at court, I was called back to court room one at 10.30am, god I was so scared again I didn't look at Mark.

I looked straight at Rosie Collins, Rosie started from where she left off the day before. I managed to answer all the question's Rosie put to me. After Rosie, Mark Shirley's defense Mr N Gerasimidis started asking me questions.

He was trying hard to turn the attack around like I'd invited Mark for coffee.

I agreed to have sex with him or perhaps it didn't happen at all, he was trying to say that I had made the whole thing up and that Cathy Marks girlfriend had given me lots of information on Mary!

I just stood as strong as I could and gave him everything that was the truth of what happened on the day in March.

A few times the judge wasn't happy with the thing's he was putting to me, I did take one break because of tears and things he was saying, eventually by lunch time I was finished on the wittness stand, the judge thanked me for being so brave.

After lunch I was allowed to sit in the court, we sat above the court room in the balconey Liz stayed with me, which was nice of her. The telephone engineer confirmed the text messages were sent quick from my phone to Mark's and from Mark's phone to mine.

They confirmed that Mark had tampered with my mobile, then the doctor came on the wittness stand, she confirmed the rape of both Mary and me, it was very hard trying to keep up with everything that was being said in court but Liz said, "Helen its all looking good, everything is on your side." she said.

I cried, "Do you think so Liz," "yes Helen its looking good," as ill as I was feeling.

My emotions were all up in the air watching Mark Shirley from where I was sat he was showing no emotion's at all.

He was just sat back on his seat like he didn't have a care in the world, I just thought why Mark, court ended for another day.

We were told to be back on Monday 9th November for Scott, Richard and Cathy to be called to the stand. Saturday and Sunday were really bad I was missing my children and they were missing me.

I didn't want to do anything over the weekend as I felt so ill, Sunday evening my sister Mandy phoned me, I could hear my children in the background they sounded really upset, my sister Mandy said "Helen the children are fine but they are missing you and Richard, I'm trying my best but they are really unhappy." "Ok, I will see if our mum will have them. I will call you back and let you know" I replied. I called my mum and told her my children sounded really upset, "mum I have a really big favour to ask you? If I were to go down to Brean Sands in Somerset to collect my children would they be able to stay at your house for the next week or so when I have to go back to court please?" My mother replied "Yes of course they can stay with me."

I rang my sister Mandy and told her that mum had agreed to have the children, so I was coming to brean to collect them.

She said "Thank God Helen as it's been really hard they are missing you so much I can't do anything with them", she said.

"How sad they all looked." We arrived at the caravan park at brean within an hour my children were overwhelmed to see mum and dad. They were all in tears; they were really pleased to see us both.

I told them they would have to stay at Nan's but they would see me in the evenings, god they were pleased.

Monday 9th November 2009, myself Richard and Scott all left for court, the mood was very quiet, Scott looked very nervous so did Richard, I felt so sick, when we got to court Liz and Deb's met us.

We were taken to the wittness support centre again. I wasn't allowed to sit with Richard or Scott as they were witness.

Deb's stayed with them, Liz sat with me. Cathy arrived she had been brought down by the police officer.

Cathy was put in a side room as she wasn't allowed to be with us. Scott was called to court one, Liz and me sat in the balcony above the court room, Scott was called to the wittness box.

He took his oath bless him with a struggle as he has a bad speech problem. Rosie Collins asked him how he knew Mark Shirley, Scott explained that he had met him a few times when Cathy was his partner.

Rosie Collins asked Scott if he could remember what happened on the 20th March, Scott replied "yes,"

"Scott can you tell the court what happened," Scott said

"He had called round to see his mum, he knocked the front door like he normally does but their was no answer,"

"Scott I'm going to stop you there" said Rosie. Rosie then asked Scott if I normally went out in the day, Scott said, "no not normally."

Rosie Collins asked Scott, "What did you do when there was no answer," Scott said

"He knocked a few times, when mum didn't answer he started to get a bit worried as I thought mum might of had a seizure,"

Rosie Collins said, "Stop their Scott." Rosie asked Scott if I suffered from seizure's, he said, "yes," "what did you do then Scott?",

Rosie Collins asked, "I looked through the window but couldn't see to good so I decided to go round the back of the house."

"Scott what happened then", Rosie asked.

Scott said "the patio door's were locked, so I banged on them and started shouting (mum are you there mum).

I noticed that all the blinds were down so I started banging on the door's again and shouted mum are you in their.

I heard something drop inside the house, it sounded a bit like something falling so I shouted again mum are you in their, my mum opened the patio doors."

Rosie then asked Scott, "What happened when your mum opened the doors," Scott said.

"That his mum seemed very strange, basically she seemed like something was wrong,"

Scott then told the court how Mark Shirley was sat at the kitchen table by the freezer, "he had a red coffee cup, I noticed my mum didn't have one,"

Mark said, "Hello Scott your mum invited me round for a coffee," Rosie asked Scott, "what happened next?"

"I said to Mark your lucky mate mum don't normally have people in when dad's at work. Mark then started talking about his bike.

I then said to Mark Im going in the living room to watch tv and eat my chips," "ok mate", Mark replied, what happened then Scott Rosie asked, "I watched home and away, about ten minutes later mum seen Mark Shirley out, I did notice that he stank of sweat as he past through the living room."

Rosie asked Scott, "How did your mum seem when she came in from seeing Mark Shirley out,"

Scott said, "She seemed very strange she just sat at the table in the kitchen, and then dad came in just before 3pm he took mum to school."

Mark's defence tried hard to break Scott's story in the wittness box, everything the defense put to Scott he answered carefully and properly.

I sat and watched my son give his evidence on my behalf, he was very brave and I felt so proud of him, Scott then joined me and Liz in the balcony.

My husband Richard was next in the wittness box, Richard took his oath, and Rosie Collins started asking Richard how he met Mark Shirley.

Richard explained that he had met Mark through our friend Cathy, Rosie Collins asked Richard what time he got home on 20th March 2009,

Richard explained that he came home about 2.50pm, he told the court how he picked our son up from school, Helen stayed in the car, after school he explained he took us to the local builder's yard Rosie asked, "How Helen seemed?" Richard replied, "She didn't really have much to say, seemed very quiet."

"What was the weekend like with Helen", Rosie Collins asked, Richard told the court that he had a really bad weekend so did the children.

"Helen at one point over the weekend told me to bugger off and packed my bags, she didn't stay in the house much she just sat in the back garden.

I asked her why her phone was so busy."

"What happened then Richard?" Rosie asked, Richard told the court that his wife Helen got really snappy with him over the phone.

She didn't want me near her everytime I tried to have a cuddle or kiss she moved away I didn't no what I had done wrong.

Rosie asked Richard when he first found out about the attack, Richard told the court that it was on the Monday Helen phoned me and said she needed to hear my voice she asked me to come home early as something had happened in the house last Friday ie:20th March 2009. Richard told the court that he left work but he was a bit late home as he met Mark Shirley on his way home, he said, "How Mark flagged him down so he had a chat with him," Rosie ask, "Richard what happened next," Richard told the court that when he got home he told Helen that he was sorry for being a bit late but Mark had flagged him down.

Helen went very pale and fell; Rosie asked Richard what happened next.

Richard told the court how Helen told him Mark Shirley had broke into their home last Friday i.e.: 20th March, Helen told Richard that Mark had done things which she couldn't explain.

She told Richard she had been to the police station with Cathy and she was waiting for them to ring her for a statement.

"How did that make you feel Richard", Rosie asked.

"Very angry and confussed I didnt really no what to think," "Richard when did you find out properly what had happened to your wife"

Rosie asked, "Towards the end of the week CID helped Helen explain some of what happened.

I still don't know the full facts as Helen had to stay pure for court, plus its hard for Helen to try and explain,"

Rosie asked, "How home life has been affected," Richard told the court how hard it has been he also told the court how his wife has changed.

Mark Shirley's defence put a few questions to Richard but Richard stayed very strong on the stand, Cathy was next to be called to the wittness box.

Sally our friend had come to court with Cathy to give us her support, Sally came and sat with us all when they called Cathy, bless Cathy she looked so nervous she took her oath and told the court her name.

Rosie Collins asked "Cathy how she met Mark," Cathy explained that she had met him through work, Rosie asked, "Cathy how did you meet Helen?"

Cathy explained that she had met Helen through the school playground as our children went to school together.

Rosie then asked, "Cathy what her relationship was like with Mark'.

Cathy said, "it was fine in the beginning, we were just friends," Rosie asked, "was Mark with someone else when you met him,".

Cathy replied, "Yes he was," Rosie asked, "did that relationship end," Cathy replied, "yes it did as me and Mark started to have a relationship."

"Cathy what was the relationship like with Mark".

"It was fine for a few months".

Rosie asked "Cathy were their problems with your family,"

Cathy replied, "a few as my mother didn't really like Mark plus I had fallen pregenant with Mark's baby".

"Cathy what was that like for you", Rosie asked.

"Very hard as Mark had been drinking alot around that time I lost the baby but Mark showed no interest," "did the relationship continue".

"Yes it did Cathy" replied.

"Is it true that you met probation with Mark," "yes a few times," "did Mark ever disclose his past to you?" Asked Rosie, "He told me about a burgalary that had gone wrong he said him and a few friends had broken into a womans house,"

"Did he tell you this in front of probation", Rosie asked, Cathy replied.

"No he never said much at probation," Rosie asked.

"Cathy did he tell you what happened at the womens house,"

"He just told me that the burgalary went wrong, his friend ran off and left him.

He told me that he tried to revive the lady but she died. He said he was aged 16 years old at the time.

He told me that, he took the wrap for the crime even though there wasn't any evidence that he had done it,"

"Cathy did you not think that was strange at the time" Rosie asked, "not really as he was only 16 years old at the time I felt sad that he had done alot of years in prison."

"I just thought everyone deserves a second chance," Rosie asked, "Cathy did Mark get arrested when he was with you from your house," "yes he did".

"What happened when he got arrested?", Rosie asked.

Cathy explained that there was an evening where she had trusted Mark to look after the children for her to go to work.

"I had a phone call from Mark later that evening to say that he had been stopped on his bike by the police he sounded very drunk he told me that the children were home on their own I rushed home from Sainsburys to find my children still asleep in their beds.

But Mark had left the back door wide open,"

"How did that make you fell Cathy" Rosie asked.

"I was angry" Cathy replied, "I had very strong words with mark over leaving my children Mark continued drinking quite a bit, a few days later Mark was ill he had a flu type bug.

He was stacked out on my sofa their was a knock at my front door it was the police, they asked if Mark Shirley was in"

I said, "Yes they then came into my house and arrested Mark for the drink driving on his bike."

"Mark didn't argue with them he just went very quietly with them," Rosie asked Cathy.

"What happened then," "I was really upset. I rang Helen to ask if she would pick the children up and come round to mine.

I asked Richard if he would ring the police station to find out what was happening the police wouldn't tell Richard as he's not Mark's family.

I left a message with probation for Marks worker to ring me the following day I managed to talk to probation and Marks worker told me that Mark had been re-called to prison because he had broken his life license rules.

"I was told that if Mark wanted to see me he would send me a visiting order," poor Cathy.

I kept thinking she looked so wore out stood in the witness box, Sally held my hand the judge ordered that it was lunch time so Cathy was aloud to leave the stand. Over lunch time Cathy wasn't allowed to be with us she had to stay on her own in the witness area, Sally our friend couldn't understand why Cathy had to stay on her own without us.

I tried to explain to Sally that it was because Cathy was a wittness.

I did feel upset for Cathy she looked so pale and scared, after lunch we went back to the court room.

Cathy was recalled to the stand; Rosie asked Cathy "Did you know that Mark Shirley was on a life license?"

"Yes", Cathy replied.

"Did that not worry you Cathy?"

"No not really as like Ive said I believed because Mark was only 16 he should have a second chance," "did you continue with the relationship Cathy,"

"Yes I did I supported Mark every step of the way."

"Is it true that you had plans to marry Mark in prison?"

"Yes", Cathy replied.

"Is it true that Mark gave his permission for his solicitor to meet with you Cathy?"

"Yes she came to my house a few times,"

"Was Helen and Richard involved in the meeting with the solicitor?"

Cathy replied, "No,"

Rosie then asked, "Cathy was it true that Mark had given permission for the solicitor to send some paperwork to your home address".

Cathy replied, "Yes it was true,"

"Cathy can you tell the court in your own words what the paper work was,"

Cathy said, "It was a dosia of Marks past crime, did you read it Cathy" Rosie asked.

"Yes I did read it," "Cathy did you share the paperwork with anyone."

Rosie asked, "Cathy said no she didn't show anyone the paperwork"

"Cathy did you show the Stockford family the paperwork."

Cathy replied, "No,"

"Did you ever talk to Helen about the paperwork or show Helen."

"No Helen didn't no anything about the paperwork I didn't tell anyone that I had Marks paperwork,"

"Why not?" Rosie asked.

Cathy said she felt to ashamed of what she had read to share it with anyone.

"Cathy is it true you made a statement for Marks parole hearing?" Rosie asked.

Cathy said, "Yes with marks solicitor."

"Did you stay in the relationship," Rosie asked.

"Yes I did," Cathy replied.

"Cathy is it true that as the months went on after the parole hearing you ended the relationship." Rosie said,

"Yes I couldn't live with what I had read I did ask Mark on a few visits at the prison if what I read was true but he kept denying it.

I asked him if he had killed the women"

He said, "No" but I didn't believe him I couldn't go against what Id read, it was hard breaking up with Mark as I really did have strong feelings for him"

"Cathy can you tell the court in your own words how you were told Mark had attacked Helen Stockford."

Cathy said, "Yes I called Helen on Monday 23rd March to ask her if she could come into my house as I had to ring probation to report some bad text messages I had from Mark over the weekend."

"Helen didn't really want to come in as we hadn't spoken properly since last November when my laptop went missing."

Helen said, "Yes it will have to be quick Cathy as, I am really busy."

"I made a coffee and rang probation I explained the text messages I passed the phone to Helen for her to speak to Fiona and Helen started asking Fiona if Mark had taken Mary's face away.

I grabbed the phone off Helen and Helen broke down Fiona told me to ring the police and make sure Helen is locked in her house."

Rosie said, "Cathy was that the first time you knew of the attack on Helen,"

Cathy replied, "Yes!"

Cathy did you at anytime give any information on Mary Wainwright to Helen,"

Cathy replied, "No."

"Thank you Cathy I have no more questions at the moment," as for me I felt heartbroken to hear that Cathy knew what he had done to that poor women.

Even thou she looked pale in the wittness box I felt ashamed of her, Marks defence stood up to talk to Cathy.

"Cathy was Mark in a relationship when he first met you,"

Cathy replied, "Yes he was,"

Mark's defence asked, "Cathy did Mark's former partner end their relationship because of you?"

Cathy said, "No" Mark had told her they had problems, "Cathy how long were you with Mark before the arrest at your house?" Cathy replied, "a few months."

"Cathy how long have you known Helen Stockford?"

Cathy replied, "A few years."

"Cathy is it true that you read the dosia before making the statements for the parole board?'

Cathy replied, "Yes! I did."

"Did you not think to end the relationship with mark after reading the dosia?"

Cathy replied, "No," why not? Marks defence asked.

Cathy said, "Because she still wanted to offer her support, but you had read about Mark,"

Cathy replied, "Yes I did."

"Cathy you made statements and gave evidence at the parole didn't you?" "Yes I did", Cathy replied.

"Is it true that Mark had a knife on him the night he got stopped for drink driving?"

Cathy said, "Yes Mark did have a small knife,"

"Cathy in your statement to the parole board did you say that the knife was yours?"

Cathy replied, "Yes I did."

"Did you give evidence at the parole board telling them that the knife was yours?"

"Yes I did."

Cathy replied, "But that was untrue wasn't it, as you tried to retrack your statements didn't you!"

Cathy replied, "Yes I did try and retrack my statements as I panicked after the parole board,"

Marks defence asked Cathy, "Was that because you knew the knife wasn't yours?"

Cathy replied, "Yes," "so Cathy could we now possibly say that you had panicked about what you read could we say that you and Helen has made all this up,"

"No!"

"But you must have shared the dosia with Helen Stockford?"

Cathy replied, "No I didn't share the dosia with Helen or anyone else."

Marks defense said, "Perhaps you and Helen had a few glasses of wine over the dosia"

Cathy replied, "No Helen didn't know about the dosia, she wasn't involved with any of it. She didn't know anything about what I've done on the parole board."

Mark's defence said, "Is it true you told Helen about Mary Wainwright? did you tell Helen what Mark had done to Mary Wainwright!"

Cathy said, "I haven't told Helen anything about Mary Wainwright as I felt too ashamed."

"Thank you Cathy I have no more questions." As for me and Richard I think we both felt Cathy had let us down as friends, even though it sounds like she didn't have much guidance from probation or Mark solicitor.

I still felt that I didn't blame Cathy for the attack but I did blame her for the lies she had told and really could not take it in my head or heart that she knew and read what he had done to Mary.

Mark's probation officer was called to the witness box, Rosie Collins asked him his name.

"Mathew", he replied.

Rosie Collins asked "Mathew if Mark was on a life license."

He replied, "Yes,"

Rosie asked, "how long have you been Mark's probation officer?"

"Not that long a few months."

"Have you met with Cathy and Mark together when they were a couple?"

Mathew replied. "Yes",

"Did at any meetings Mark disclose his past history to Cathy?"

Mathew replied, "No Mark didn't disclose his crime to Cathy at any meetings?"

Rosie asked, "Why doesn't workers from probation help with disclosure?"

Mathew said, "It was policy that all offenders should disclose to partners themselves. It's not something that probation would do for them."

Rosie asked, About Mark's heavy drinking were there not risks around heavy drinking "Isn't it part of the license conditions that he wasn't allowed to drink."

Mathew said, "Unfortunately risk can never be eliminated entirely but we do try and supervise offenders as much as we can in the community."

Rosie ask, "if it was procedure for partners to be allowed paperwork if the offender gives her permission," Mathew said, "he could not comment on the paperwork as he wasn't sure," "no further questions thank you."

Mark's defence asked a few questions, the judge then thanked Mathew and told him to step down.

Cathy came up and joined us in the court; I asked her if she was alright.

She said, "Yes" and went and sat next to Sally, Richard and Liz were very good they kept asking me if I was ok.

Mark Shirley was called to the stand, god I paniced they opened the glass proof door and he just walked through the court to the witness stand.

Richard held my hand tight; I felt so sick and shaken I didnt think and wasn't told that he would come out that way.

Mark Shirley took his oath in his Welsh accent.

Rosie asked him his name, "Mark Shirley", he replied, "Mark do you understand why you were recalled back to prison?" Rosie asked poor behavior.

Mark replied, "Id been drinking alot,"

"Did you commit a crime back in 1987?" Rosie asked.

Mark said, "Not on my own no", "but Mark there is no evidence to sugest that anyone was with you.

The two named boys that you gave in your statement at the time were checked and cleared by the police weren't they."

Mark said "No."

Rosie asked, "But it is true that you broke into Mary Wainwright's flat back in 1987 in Wales."

Mark said 'No."

"Did you break in to Mary Wainwright's flat and ransack it to then rape and kill her."

Mark replied no, "but you did after killing her you put a 2p piece and a knife on her body," again Mark said "No,"

Rosie then asked, "Mark if it was true that he had serverly injured Mary's face,"

"Is that why you covered her face," Mark said.

"No I can maintain to this day that I didn't murder Mrs Wainwright."

Rosie then asked, "Mark if he had a relationship with Cathy"

Mark said, "Yes I did," Rosie asked, "Was the relationship going well," "Yes".

Mark replied, "Were you recalled back to prison when you were with Cathy for drinking and having a knife?"

Mark said, "Yes,".

"Mark did Cathy support you with prison,"

Mark said, "Yes."

"Mark did Richard and Helen support you at that time."

Mark replied, "Yes in the beginning"

"Mark did you allow Cathy to have the dosia to read"

Mark said, "Yes he did."

Rosie asked, "Mark if Cathy had made statement's for the parole board."

Mark said, "Yes Cathy did."

"Mark is it fair to say Cathy covered you in those statements with the knife."

Mark replied, "Yes I asked her to."

Rosie then asked, "Mark if Cathy had asked him if he had murdered Mary Wainwright."

Mark said, "yes Cathy did ask me a few times but I told her no because I didn't kill her,"

I just sat in that court looking at Mark Shirley thinking how low can you get just standing there under oath telling very cold lies, it was like he had no remorse for what he had done to Me and Mary.

The judge ordered the case closed for today.

That evening as we came away from the court I really felt ill, I couldn't take in what I had heard over the day.

I was so upset I went into Cathy's house where I just broke down in a very big way and I shouted and cried at Cathy, "why didn't you tell me you knew that poor women had no face, you knew what he had done and yet you didn't tell me, why Cathy, why didn't you tell me."

"Helen Im so sorry", Cathy said.

"I couldn't tell you because of court"

"Cathy is that why you and Fiona acted so quick in the beginning of all this,"

Cathy said, "Yes that is why."

Sally our friend made me a coffee, bless her she held me so tight when I first went into Cathy's house. When I got home from Cathy's I just couldn't rest.

I felt so sad for Mary's family and mine, Richard and Scott they looked so ill, I felt so sad as I hadn't seen much of my children.

The following morning we all left for court, Cathy and Sally came in our car, when we all arrived at court we all went straight through to the witness area, Cathy and Sally sat together.

Liz and Debs were their they were talking to Richard and Scott we all had coffee, then we all made our way up to courtroom one, Mark Shirley was called to the witness stand, again he was bought through the court from behind the glass panel's.

Rosie Collins said, "Mark Shirley did you know Helen and Richard Stockford for very long,"

Mark replied, "Not that long."

"How did you meet them" Rosie asked

Mark replied, "I met them when I started my relationship with Cathy."

"Mark Shirley, you told the court yesterday that the Stockford's supported you when you were recalled to prison for drinking,"

Mark said "yes they did,"

Rosie asked, "Mark Shirley did you ever tell the Stockford's your past crime."

Mark replied, "No!"

Rosie asked, "Mark Shirley had you seen very much of the Stockford's family since you were released."

Mark replied, "No I hadn't seen Helen in a long time Ive waived to Richard if I have seen him out in his car."

"Mark Shirley is it true that you called to the Stockford's home one evening in March, what reason did you have to call on them?"

Mark replied, "I went to there house to let them no I was sorting out my bike with Cathy."

Rosie asked, "Mark Shirley did you break into Helen Stockford's house on the 20th March this year."

Mark replied, "No I didn't break in, Helen phoned me a a few days before and said even thou her and Cathy had fallen out it did not mean, I couldn't go round for a coffee and a chat."

Rosie said, "Mark Shirley you are telling the court that Mrs Stockford said you could go round for coffee is that right."

Mark replied, "Yes".

"So you are telling the court Mark Shirley that you were at Helen Stockford's house on the 20th March this year."

Mark replied "Yes".

Rosie asked, "Mark Shirley what happened on the 20th of March when you went to Helen Stockford's house?"

Mark Shirley told the court that he visited Helen Stockford, "We had a coffee together and a general chat."

Rosie said, "What sort of things did you talk about."

Mark replied, "It was just a general chit-chat."

"Mark Shirley did you talk about Mary Wainwright, did you tell Helen Stockford how you killed Mary."

Mark replied, "No I didnt tell Helen about Mrs Wainwright."

Rosie said, "But didn't you tell Helen Stockford that you had killed Mary, because you wanted to kill Helen in the same way that you had killed Mary didnt you?"

Mark replied "No."

Rosie said but you did kill Mary Wainwright.

Mark said, "No."

Rosie said, "But you did rape and abuse Helen Stockford thinking that she was Mary didnt you."

Mark replied, "No."

Rosie said, "But Mark Shirley you did rape and abuse Mary Wainwright untill you had killed her didnt you."

Mark Shirley, replied "No."

Rosie then asked, "Mark Shirley is it true that you left a two pence piece and a knife on Mary Wainwright's body, were you getting angry because you didn't have the same things to put on Helen Stockford's body the day you attacked her,"

Mark replied, "No I didn't"

Mark also said, "When I was in the flat in Wales I tripped over her while, I was walking through the bedroom and fell on the body, I got off and ran out the flat I didn't see any knife or two pence piece on her body when I fell on top of her."

Rosie asked, "Mark can you explain how your D.N.A got on Mary Wainwright's body."

Mark replied, "I was on the body for 10 seconds before I got up and ran and left the flat."

Rosie then said "Mark Shirley the D.N.A was all over Mary Wainwright's body and it has been proven by the pathologist report also the knife and the two pence piece were positioned on Mary Wainwright's abduman, if you had fallen on the body they would have fallen off and not still be in that position on the body, can you explain this?"

Mark replied, "No!"

Rosie said, "No more question's Mark Shirley."

Mark's defence stood up to talk, Marks' defence asked, "Mark Shirley did Helen Stockford invite you to her house for coffee"

Mark replied "yes, she phoned me."

Mark's defence asked, "Mark Shirley did you at anytime tell Helen Stockford that you had raped and abused and killed Mary Wainwright"

Mark replied, "No"

Marks defence then asked, "Mark Shirley how do you think Helen Stockford knew about Mary Wainwright then"

Mark replied, "I think Helen heard it through a close friend"

Mark's defence then asked, "Mark Shirley who do you believe that close friend might be?"

Mark replied, "Cathy"

Mark's defence then said, "Mark Shirley you agree that you were at Helen Stockford's house on the 20th March this year"

Mark replied, "Yes I was."

Mark's defence then said, "Mr Shirley did you attack and rape Helen Stockford on the day in question,"

Mark Shirley told the court "no attack took place", Mark's defence said, "Mr Shirley why do you think Helen Stockford has said these things about you,"

Mark replied, "I don't know I have done nothing wrong I dont no why these things have been said about me unless they are trying to stick me back in prison"

Mark's defence then said, "Mr Shirley how has all this made you feel,"

"Shocked by the allegations I have done nothing wrong," "no more questions Mr Shirley thank you," the judge told Mark Shirley he could step down.

Court ended for the day, I was so upset, Mark Shirley was really trying to make the court believe he had done nothing wrong to Mary or me, why cant he just tell the truth he's so cold looking in the face as he talks about Mary and me.

It was a very long night, the following day we all went to court, I think we were all feeling very tired and worn out, both barrister's had to give their summing up to the jury, we went up to the court room one. Rosie stood and faced the jury!

The idea of us or our loved ones would be the subject of sexual attacks in the street would be probably be one of our collective greatest fears, to be the subject of a serious sexual assault in the privacy of our own home, within the comfort, security and hub of your family life is probably one of anyones greatest nightmares.

March 20th to (Helen Stockford) at the hands of this defendant, was her greatest nightmare.

Mark Shirley targeted her in her own home and he abused her in quite the most repulsive of ways. Rosie then told the jury that she had given them everything including the case of Mary Wainwright.

"No more to say my lord," Rosie sat down.

Mark's defence stood up and turned to the jury, "you have all heard that Mark Shirley had been engaged to the alledged victims best friend, the alledged victim exchanged text messages with Mark Shirley on the morning of the rape, you have also heard that she only knew about the details of the murder committed by Mark Shirley in 1987 because her friend had told her.

Mark Shirley is faced with one count of rape, one count of false imprisonment, three counts of assault but penetration and one account of committing a sexual offence, Marks defence thanked the jury and sat down.

Court ended for the day. The night was really bad I didn't know what to think or feel my emotions were all over the place, on Friday 13th November we went back to court, myself and Richard sat in the witness area with our son Scott, Debs and Liz.

Debs said, "Helen it will be ok your see, you have everything supporting you don't look so worried."

Debs and Liz explained that the media would be outside after court today so we think it might be a good idea for you and Richard to make two statements; one for a guilty plea and one for a not guilty plea, Richard agreed we all helped him make both statements.

Will White came into see us, "How's it going Helen are you ok?"

"Yes", I replied.

We agreed with Liz and Debs that today in court was private as a family. Debs spoke to Cathy and Sally to explain to them that they had to sit in the lower court room today. Cathy she got so upset, but I had to be with CID, Richard and Scott.

Plus, I knew in my head and heart there was a lot more to tell about my attack, but I felt it was too late now, plus I didn't think CID would believe me.

I promised myself that there was a certain part of my attack which I would have to keep private however hard I would take this part that I haven't told to my grave

We were all called to court room one, from the balcony of court one I could see Cathy and Sally, they brought Mark Shirley in behind the glass panel.

The judge spoke to the jury; he told them that they had heard from both barristers. They were told to retire, the jury left the court. God I felt sick and ill, we walked around town for a while over lunchtime, I remember feeling really scared, I kept thinking what if they dont believe me. We headed back to the court had a coffee in the witness area, Debs and Liz were trying hard to keep the mood's up in us all.

Eventually we were called to court one, as the jury were comming back in. Again Cathy and Sally had to sit in the lower part of court, I remember looking across at Mark, he had his head down and he looked grey in colour.

The jury came in; they were asked if they had reached a verdict, yes my lord.

The first charge was read out, that being false imprisonment, how do you find the defendant "guilty"!

The next charge was called out, that being rape, how do you find the defendant "guilty"!

The next charge was called out, that being three counts of assault by penetration, how do you find the defendant, "guilty" on three accounts, the next charge was called out, that being committing false imprisonment, how do you find the defendant "guilty"!

The next charge was called out, that being with the intention of committing a sexual offence, how do you find the defendant "guilty"!

My head was thumping all I could hear was Mark Shirley on one side saying they won't believe you! And on the other side I could hear guilty plea!

I just cried silent tears. I managed to look down at Mark Shirley he was shaking uncontrolably, I got up from my seat with the noise in my head and I ran from the court balcony down the court corridor. Liz came after me, Helen are you alright, they have found him guilty. I remember saying to Liz that they believed me.

Liz took me back in the court, where I heard the judge saying he considered Shirley to be a very dangerous man. The judge asked for a full report before sentencing him on the 16th December 2009.

The judge also said that he was considering sentencing Shirley once again to life. The judge remanded Shirley into custody untill the 16th December 2009.

We were taken into a side room, when we came out of court, CID and Rosie Collins were so pleased that Mark Shirley was found guilty of all count's. They said that they would prefer us to wait to speak to the media untill we came back for the sentence.

They assured myself and Richard that Mark should get life, "we dont feel Mark will be let out again, Helen."

"Thank you Rosie", I said, I felt so numb inside, my head was banging, when we left court we told the media we had no comment at this time.

When we got home, I felt really tired, my whole body inside didn't feel real my head didn't feel like it belonged to me.

Richard held me, "are you ok babe?"

He said, I replied, "Yes."

Richard asked if I wanted anything to eat, no not at the moment I replied, Richard made a drink.

I rang the children; they were very pleased when I told them Mark had been found guilty! Can we all come home now mum asked my daughter Amy, not tonight darling, mum will have you all in the morning.

I gave my children a kiss over the phone and said to them I loved them all very much and then said goodnight. Richard had the t.v on, he said, "babe are you ok, its all over the news,"

I replied, "Im fine Richard Im going to have a bath,"

Richard said, "Ok."

When I got into the bath I started to scrub, I felt guilty for Mary's family because poor Mary's name was all over the news. I felt very hurt and angry because there was a big part of me inside that was hopeing that Mark Shirley was going to admit his guilt for Mary and myself. Plus in my head it still felt like he was telling me no one will believe you if you tell.

When I got out of the bath, Cathy text me, "are you ok Helen please come round mine."

I said to Richard, "Cathy want's me to go round her's to see her and Sally."

Richard said, "It's up to you babe."

When I went round Cathy, Sally opened the front door, she put her arms round me, "well done Helen", she said through her tears. Cathy gave me a hug

"Im so sorry Helen," Cathy said

"Helen I feel so guilty for what I've done," I just looked at her (Helen) Cathy said, "do you blame me for what I've done,"

I told Cathy that I didn't blame her for the attack but at the moment I did blame her for what she had done wrong, "just give me some time Cathy", I said.

Sally asked me if I wanted coffee or a glass of wine.

"Sally", I said, "I will have a coffee with you both but then Im going home." When I got home Richard asked me if I was ok

"Yes", I replied "(Helen) you weren't very long,"

"No", I replied, "I can't be bothered Richard Im feeling to ill to sit and talk to the both"

Liz phoned me a few time's over the week's just to make sure that things were ok. I was asked by the Bristol Evening Post if I would give them my comment on Mark Shirley, I told the man from Evening Post that I would let him know shortly as I needed to talk to my husband. Richard and myself discussed what I should do about giving my views of what's happened on the 20th March 2009.

I told Richard that I felt very strong about waiveing my name, I told Richard I wanted to do this because I felt poor Mary Wainwright never had a chance, I felt I owed this explanation to Mary's family.

I just wanted her family to at least know my name, Richard agreed with me. I rang Geoff Bennett as he was the reporter that sat behind me at court.

I agreed with Geoff that I would go to the Evening Post on the 15th December 2009, which was tomorrow the day before court.

Geoff thanked me he said, "I will look forward to meeting with you." The following day we took the children to school, we then went straight down to the Evening Post building.

Geoff met with us, I told Geoff that I had decided to waive my name, I managed to tell Geoff why I felt so strong about doing this.

Geoff said, "Helen that's a really brave thing your doing," so on the 15th December 2009 I waived my name and gave a full exclusive to Geoff Bennett at Bristol Evening Post.

The full exclusive went to print that day ready for the 16th December 2009, the sentencing day for Mark Shirley.

## *Sentencing For Mark Shirley 16<sup>th</sup> December 2009*

On the 16<sup>th</sup> December 2009, I took my children to my mums house early, Richard and myself got ready for court, the mood in the house was very quite, I felt really nervous, I really didn't want to go back down to the Bristol Crown Court as I really didn't want to see Mark Shirley.

Cathy text me, "how are you feeling Helen,"

I text her back saying, "terrified Cathy," she then texted me to ask if there was any chance they could have a lift please.

I text Cathy back and said, "Yes that's ok."

When we got to court Liz and Debs were there waiting, on our way in the court we over looked the media setting up their cameras.

We went straight into the witness area. Richard and I, had to go in a side room with CID as they wanted to talk to us.

Scott came with us we were told that Rosie would talk to us after the sentence was passed. We were also told that there was a media conference being held at feeder road CID head quarters after court.

CID said they would have to escort us to the conference. Will White came in to see if we were all ok, "how are you doing Helen?"

I replied, "Nervous Will but I'm trying to stay calm,"

Will said, "has Liz explained everything to you all Helen, do you have any questions,"

I replied, "no Will, Liz has explained everything thank's."

We were called to court room one, my legs were like stone, Richard held my hand, "he said are you ok Helen,"

"Yes", I replied. Liz and Debs sat at the top part of the court like before with us, I didn't have the courage to look down at Mark Shirley. The judge came in the court and sat down; he told Mark Shirley that he could remain seated. The judge started to read out his sentencing speech. I got to be honest with you all I just felt sick and ill. To hear part of the evidence again it was all to much for me their were times that I couldn't hear at all, I was blocking out what the judge was saying, my mind had become blank, before I knew it the sentence had been passed.

When we came out of the court room, we were taken to the side room. Richard and Me thanked CID for their support, Rosie Collins came into the room to talk to us, she was explaining the sentence that Mark had been given.

I got to be honest I wasn't really taking it in, my head was just thumping.

Richard said, "He wasn't happy with the 9 yrs tariff."

I said to Rosie, "You all said he would get life and never come out of prison again."

Rosie replied, "The judge had to cut the sentence by half Helen but I dont think he will come out of prison again."

Richard said, "But we can't be sure."

Richard then asked about the statement he made at the trial, CID passed him the statement as we were leaving the side room.

Richard asked if he could change it, but there was no time as we were walking out of court in a hurry, and before we knew it we were infront of the media, Richard was told to read his statement, a reporter asked me!

"Helen is Mary stood with you today"

I replied, "Very much so,"

"Helen are you happy with today's sentence?"

I replied, "no I dont feel justice has been done properly," probation then pushed our son into the side of me and CID started to walk forward we were pushed through the media crowd and marched down the road into the CID car.

I asked Liz if we were going to feeder road.

Liz replied, "No it's been cancelled." The journey home was silent; they dropped us outside our house.

Liz said, "I will be in touch Helen."

As a victim I felt very let down, as a family I don't think we will ever understand why we were treated so badly.

# *Sentence*

AT 10:35am
16TH DECEMBER 2009

JUDGE: "Mr Shirley you remain seated."

In 1987, when you were 16, you broke into the house of a 67-year old widow called Mary Wainwright. She, it would appear, was subjected to an awful ordeal by you. The injuries, in particular to her face, were horrific. She eventually choked on her own blood. It is plain from the evidence that emerged in your recent trial that at some stage you had sexual intercourse with her wearing a condom because you did not leave any forensic sign of sexual intercourse, but the pathological evidence demonstrated that her injuries were consistent with such. It is clear from what you told Helen Stockford that you had sex with that 67-year-old widow and you were confident that you had left no trace that could be linked to you.

Other forensic evidence in this case, in particular the evidence in relation to fibres, was extremely cogent and demonstrated that you had been in contact with Mary Wainwright for sufficient time to leave such forensic signs. You told Helen Stockford that you moved Mary Wainwright around her flat before eventually she died, and you remembered her gasping last breath. You subsequently were to pretend that it was not you who killed her but another who had broken into her flat with you. Anyone examining the totality of the evidence easily came to the conclusion that your story was but a pretence. In your trial at Cardiff Crown Court you started to give evidence. You had been cross-examined for 20 mins when the proceedings came to an end for the day. It was an uncomfortable 20 minutes because you had few answers of any validity. The following day you decided not to return to the witness box.

You have, over the years since your release--for you were released having served 16 years--maintained that deceitful story about the murder of Mary Wainwright. You maintained it untill the day in March when you got into Helen Stockford's house and sat yourself at the kitchen table. She came down and she noticed that the blinds in the conservatory had been pulled down; they were never down usually. You pulled them down because of what you had in mind. She asked you what you were doing there. You said that you had come for coffee.

What followed over the next three hours was a grotesque ordeal for her. You told her that she was a nice lady and you could trust her. You told her that there was another lady who you had trusted and who had trusted you. You said she was a sweet lady and her name was Mary. You told Helen Stockford that you had watched, Mary for some time.

You then took a knife from your waistband. You got her to remove her top. With the knife you then cut two triangular sections from the front of her bra where her nipples would be. She was completely terrified. She had to listen to you talking about Mary. She attempted to persuade you that it would be a good idea to drive to Cardiff to see where she lived, or to see her. She having attempted in that way to get you out of the house, and you not falling for it.

You got her on to the table, and you removed the rest of her clothing. You kept saying to her that Mary smelt good and that Helen Stockford did not smell as sweet as Mary. You told her how you had defaced Mary and, indeed you had.

You described how you had kicked Mary's face. You seemed to be laughing to yourself as you descibed Mary's last breath. You spoke of leaving Mary's body a two-pence coin and an ornamental knife, and so you had. You spoke of wheather or not to cut her nipple off or her breast off. You got her to position herself on the table so that her breast were over the edge of it. Helen Stockford described in moving terms how difficult it was to get into that position at knife-point as she was shaking very badly.

You appeared to find it funny that the arms of her jumper, which she still had on the top, made it look as though she had four arms as her arms were stretched out. You drew your knife over different parts of her body. She felt the coldness of the knife down between her thighs. You told her that you wanted to make her smell as sweet as Mary. You sniffed the front part of her breasts. There came a time when you put the knife in her anus.

She said it felt cold and painful and horrible. You talked to her about which parts of her lower body would smell best if you were to make them bleed. You talked about which way the blood were to flow on the floor. You told her that Friday was a good day for drinking and killing - and this was a Friday. You got her to kneel up with her backside in the air. You got behind her and you entered her from the rear in her anus. You did that on about four occasions, and she believed that you were wearing a condom. It was at that stage that you told her that you had sex with Mary but it was not unprotected sex. This ordeal went on and on. You pulled her head back by the hair when you were having anal sex with her.

She thought that on the first occasion it lasted about 20 minutes. You put your fingers, or finger, in her vagina at one stage--count 4--and in her anus, count 5. She believed that she was going to be killed and at one stage suggested that you should get on and kill her if that was what you were proposing to do. You ran the knife over the back of her kneck, and you talked about which way her head would roll when it hit the floor and how much blood would be to play in. She was unable to control her bowel function and you appeared to enjoy further humiliating her by wiping her faeces over her in part. It was perhaps extremely fortunate for Helen Stockford that her son came around to her house. He could not get in initially, and that was because the doors were locked and the conservatory blinds were down, and you ensured that she got dressed and you ensured through veiled threats that she would not disclose what you had done to her.

Nor did she for a few days.

It is abundantly plain from the history of this case that she was very severely traumatised indeed. No-one who sat through her evidence could have been in any doubt that she was bravely recounting the most horrific ordeal that many people could imagine. She did so with courage and with dignity.

Your case was that it was a fiction and was a conspiracy between her and your former partner to ensure that you returned to prison. Your case and your evidence was a palpable lie. Your sentence is not increased because of that, but you have no credit for a plea of guilty. You are, in my judgment, a highly dangerous and evil man. I find that you are dangerous within the meaning of the 2003 Criminal Justice Act.

I have to consider what sentence should be passed upon you. These offences, sexual, sexual offences, were very serious indeed. They amounted to repeated rapes.

The aggravating circumstances were numerous. The sentencing guideline, council guideline for such activity suggests a starting point of

15 years custody. I conclude that after a trial I would have passed a total sentence covering the various offences of 18 years, but I am satisfied that there should be an indeterminate sentence in this case and that that should be a life sentence with a minimum term of nine years, which is half the 18 years that I have specified.

I make it clear that I am obliged by parliament to halve the figure of 18 years. It is not a matter of judicial discretion, it is something determined by the executive and not by judges. I am satisfied that these offences are so serious as to justify a life sentence, and I do so having very much in mind the circumstances of your previous offence of murder; that murder, in the context of what emerged during your trial, of rape of Mary Wainwright during the course of your offending. It is not clear from the forensic evidence or from your account whether she was still alive when you had sex with her. There were some forensic indications that she may already have been dead.

The sentence on you is one of life imprisonment with a minimum term of nine years.

"Miss Collins, is there anything else that needs deaking with?"

MISS COLLINS: "My lord, no. He will, of course, should he ever be released, be required to sign the sex offenders register. But that is a notification requirement."

JUDGE: "Yes."

"Very well, you may go down.
11:00am"

Page last updated at 14:42 GMT, Wednesday, 16 December 2009

✉ E-mail this to a friend     🖶 Printable version

# Murder re-enactment rapist jailed

**A convicted murderer has been jailed for life for raping a woman seven months after he was released from prison on parole.**

Mark Shirley, 39, subjected Helen Stockford, from Bristol, to degrading and humiliating abuse before the rape.

In attacking Mrs Stockford, 40, who has waived her right to anonymity, he tried to re-enact elements of a murder he had committed in Cardiff 22 years before.

Mark Shirley was found guilty of his latest crime last month

Shirley was described by the judge as a highly dangerous man.

He is recommended to serve a minimum of nine years.

Shirley was first jailed for life in 1987, when 16, for murdering a pensioner.

He was found guilty last month of rape, false imprisonment, serious sexual assault, and committing false imprisonment with the intention of committing a sexual offence at Bristol Crown Court.

In the latest attack Mrs Stockford, a mother-of-five, was held at knifepoint for three-and-a-half hours at her home.

Shirley had been convicted of murdering Mary Wainwright, 67, whose disfigured body was found in her flat in Llanrumney, Cardiff in 1987.

Helen Stockford talks about her feelings after the court case

She had been beaten and stabbed and there were ritualistic features to the killing.

Shirley was later jailed for life at Cardiff Crown Court for that murder, but released on parole after 16 years in 2003.

He was later twice recalled to prison for excessive drinking and for carrying a knife but re-released in August 2008.

Seven months after his second release from prison, on 20 March, he raped Ms Stockford in north Bristol, attacking her with a flick-knife.

> 66 We only wish that he would have some remorse as to what he has done previously and now 99
>
> Richard Stockford, husband of Shirley's victim

She gave evidence to the trial jury, saying Shirley told her she was a trusting and sweet lady "like Mary".

For three hours Shirley told her what he had done to Mary Wainwright - the first time he has ever admitted his guilt to anyone.

Mrs Stockford was so terrified that she begged him to kill her quickly. It was only when her son returned home unexpectedly that she escaped with her life.

She left court on Wednesday saying Mary Wainwright was in her thoughts. She said she believed that Shirley should never have been let out of jail.

Mrs Stockford's husband Richard said: "With today's verdict we feel that justice has been done and that this man has been put behind bars once and for all.

"We only wish that he would have some remorse as to what he has done previously and now."

The judge Mr Justice Royce commended Mrs Stockford for her bravery and dignity in bringing Shirley to justice.

The Parole Board, which made the decision to release Shirley from prison, is to carry out a review of the case.

But the Probation Service said that they had followed all procedures and that they could only manage risk, never eliminate it.

# GETTING OVER CHRISTMAS

On the 23rd of December 2009, Deb's from next link rang to say, "hi Helen hows it going with you all," I replied, "not to good Deb." "Do you want me to come up to your's Helen," "please Deb if you can fit me in," "I will be up to you in about an hour." Lisa from CID rang me to say, "Hi Helen is it ok if I come up to your's with the camera man, as we have to take the cameras off the house." I didn't really know what to say to Lisa.

So I just said, "Yes." When Deb arrived we started to talk, I explained to Deb how we were treated at court. Deb agreed that it was bad, but she didn't no why we were treated that way. As we were talking, Richard had let Lisa in with the camera man.

"Hi Helen how's you", Lisa said, "not to good at the moment", I replied. Lisa said, "Helen well Im here," "I better tell you mark Shirley has the right of a 28 days appeal against the sentence." I looked at Lisa and said, "do I have the right of a 28 day appeal as Im not happy with the sentence," Lisa made no comment, apart from she had to see if the camera man had finished. I think Deb's felt embarrased, I ask her, "what shall I do," "I don't know Debs", replied.

As the day went on Richard and me didnt no what to think, we both had a really bad night, I was really upset, why didn't Lisa answer me I kept thinking. Christmas eve, poor Richard he was trying to make the day as good as he could for me and the children, I tried as hard as I could to make the day special for them. The pain inside me was killing me, but I didn't want to let it show to Richard or the children.

The children went out for an hour with Richard; I guess that was to get a small gift for me. Cathy text me she was really excited as she was doing Christmas dinner for her whole family. She was having her mum and her sister plus her ex husband, and a few family friends. She was excited because she was going to be laying out her big table with all the trimmings on it, As for me I felt sad because I only had the small round table with four chairs that CID had brought us in replacement of my big farm house table.

I also felt very sad because I still hadn't heard from my sister. I only got small updates. I only got small updates if my mum popped in to see me, I was very much hopeing that she might ring me Christmas day, as it was getting very close to her moving to Australia. When the children got back they were so excited, they were all looking forward to there present's on Christmas day. God it was really hard trying to keep the mood up inside me, as for Richard I felt he done us all proud. Christmas morning my children got up so excited, Richard went round my mother's house to collect her. When she arrived the children started to open the presents.

They were all so very pleased with what we had bought them. I started to prepare lunch Richard set up the wii on the t.v my mum and Richard started playing with the children, even thou I was trying hard to enjoy the day with my family, my heart was somewhere else, I kept thinking about Mary and what sort of Christmas her family were haveing. Lunch wasn't to bad we didn't have much in the way of a table to trim, but we managed. After lunch, we had plenty of fun playing bowling on the wii. Throughout the day Cathy's children came round to show me what they had got for Christmas, Amy my eldest daughter was in her bedroom showing Cathy eldest daughter what she had for Christmas, I could hear them laughing. I felt so warm inside as I hadn't heard the girls laughing together for months.

That is when I decided for the sake of all the children Cathy's and mine, it wasn't worth putting a wedge between the two family's. I no deep down I can never forgive Cathy for what she has done, but she has tried to put things right by offering her full support with court, Later that evening my mother went home.

"Thanks mum", I said as she was leaving. Richard and me started talking about what Lisa had told me, Richard said, "surley babe you should have 28 days to appeal if Mark has," "I dont no", I replied, Richard said, "what if we were to look on the internet," "we can try it", I said.

All over Christmas Richard searched the internet, we didn't really have a clue what sort of things we were looking at, it was very frustrating because it was Christmas and no department was open for us to get some guidance. Trying to do Christmas for our children was really hard when we also had to try and sort out what right I have as a victim.

# FIGHTING FOR JUSTICE

Over the Christmas period most places were closed to get advice, Richard was working really hard on the internet.

He was trying to find out my right's of the 28 days appeal against the sentence, Mark Shirley had been given, as we felt the sentence was to lenient, being lay people we worked out 28 days from the sentence date, but we worked it out on working day's because that is what the online solicitor advised us at this time.

We were not aware that the attorney general worked over holiday time and we were not aware at the time it was a sraight 28 days that didn't include weekend's. Richard and myself worked it out to be that we had enough time to write to everyone. Richard had found lots of people in the government to write to, plus we thought we would write to C.P.S. probation services and parole in hopes that I might get some help to appeal the sentence Mark Shirley was given.

I was so worried about Mark placing an appeal and me having nothing in place. Richard and me worked out with no professional help that I had untill 22-1-2010 to lodge an appeal, over a few evenings as wore out as we both felt we managed to complete a letter for everyone, we sent 55 letters out between all the different departments in hope that government probation, parole and cps might be able to help me appeal Mark Shirley's sentence and guide me through a 28 days appeal.

Mrs Helen Stockford
Mr Richard Stockford
12<sup>th</sup> jan 2010

To Whom it may concern,

You may have seen or heard about the recent COPYCAT RAPIST TRIAL in November 2009, I am HELEN STOCKFORD the victim, I can't believe this man has been given 28 days to appeal against his sentence as it has been a horrendous time for myself and my family with the ordeal I have been through already.

I am very disappointed in the sentencing of MARK SHIRLEY, considering the six charges of: Fasle imprisonment, Commiting an offence with intent to committ a sexual offence, Rape and three charges of assult by penetration.

Plus, his past history regarding ritualised murder of a 66yr old widow MARY WAINWRIGHT in Cardiff South Wales in 1987. MARK SHIRLEY was convicted for this murder in January 1987, He was given a life sentence and came out on parole after 16yrs, Since his parole their has been lots of issues regarding his recalls due to alchol which has all taken place since being allowed parole in 2003, Which has really made me and my family feel disappointed with the legal system.

To think this cold brutal man wasn't watched by probation ie; Weekly contact, He was living life to it's full just waiting for another victim to attack so he could re-live what he had done to MARY WAINWRIGHT all over again.

I feel as a victim I am very lucky MARK SHIRLEY didn't kill me like MARY WAINWRIGHT, he just put me through such a terrifying ordeal in my home, That has left me feeling that justice has not been done, As he only got life with 9 years tariff.

So this is why I am asking for your help and support because as a victim with a family I really firmly believe that MARK SHIRLEY has been given enough chances with parole, He didn't sort himself out after killing MARY WAINWRIGHT.

He lived life to its full since 2003 but part of his lience should have been NO drinking of alchol, NO threatening behaviour, NO knives and yet he has acheived all of this and managed to attack again where he has tried very hard to copy what he had done in JANUARY 1987 to MARY WAINWRIGHT so could you help me appeal against this please and give me and my family JUSTICE and THE COMMUNITY we should all have a right to feel safe in our HOMES and in THE COMMUNITY, SO PLEASE DON'T ALLOW THIS MAN A THIRD CHANCE AND ATTACK AGAIN HE HAD HIS CHANCES AND THE THIRD CHANCE COULD MEAN DEATH FOR ANOTHER LADY

As the JUDGE agreed he was a VERY DANGEROUS MAN and he should give him life with out parole but he had follow the guide lines of the LAWS. MARY WAINWRIGHT died through his EVIL HAND'S.

For myself YES he came CLOSE to KILLING ME. He is an EVIL MAN THAT SHOULD GET LIFE WITHOUT PAROLE.

Im not only sending this letter to yourselves Im also sending it to THE EUROPEAN COURTS OF APPEAL as I feel so strongly about this sentence as JUSTICE HAS NOT BEEN DONE. The Bristol C P S & C.I.D dealt with this case & The BARRISTER was ROSSALINE COLLINS, they all assured me and my family that MARK SHIRLEY would get LIFE WITH NO PAROLE but they didnt mention until the 23RD DECEMBER 2009 that he had 28 DAYS TO APPEAL.

We have found this very disturbing & upsetting and can't believe this is happening.

Please E -mail me if you have received this letter.


Yours Sincerley
Helen Stockford & Richard Stockford

Richard also sent email's of the same letter to all departments, I really felt this was unfair I had gone through so much with the attack and the trial, so had my family and here we are trying to work out what right I had as a victim it really hurt me that Lisa had told me about Mark's 28 day appeal rights and yet she didn't answer me when I ask if I had 28 days to appeal.

Emotionally I felt so low but I knew I had to try and find out what my right's were as I didnt want Shirley to come back out of prison. I also managed to sign a contract with southwest news, I gave a full exclusive to the mail and I had signed two contracts one with pick me up magazine and one with new magazine.

Richard had also managed to set up a facebook campaign, the technical man from southwest news had sent through some really good campaign logo's for it. I was really taken back by the support people were giving us, we had people from all over the world, there messages really touched my heart, also with out me knowing Richard had worked very hard to find Mary's resting place because he knew how sad I felt for her and her family.

When Richard told me I was really taken back inside as I now felt I could maybe take flowers or something for her. Over the next few weeks while I was waiting for replies from the letter we had sent to everyone I manage to send a couple of emails to CID.

I asked Lisa if she could advise me if I had the same right as Mark (ie) 28 days to appeal, Lisa sent me back an email saying why would you want to do that, I didn't really no what to think at the time, strange reply I thought, so I sent her another email saying that I was not happy with the sentence Mark got, did I have the same right's as him to lodge a 28 days appeal, Lisa sent another email to say what do you want to appeal, so I emailed Will White head of CID in my case to ask him if I had the right of a 28 day appeal.

I asked him for my crime ref number, he told me to contact C.P.S. I managed to get hold of C.P.S who I gave all my details to including the ref number to be told there is a letter in the post for you Mrs Stockford. There was a big part of me inside that felt releaved, At last I thought. The letter arrived on the 22nd January 2010.

The letter read: Dear Mrs Stockford your letter dated 12 January together with your email dated 13th January 2010 have been passed to me for my attention by the chief crown prosecutor Mr Hughes, May I first of all express my sympathy for the terrible ordeal that you have suffered and concern at your disappointment in the legal system.

I can only trust that the passage of time will go some way to ease the distress and that I can take some steps to provide you with a more detailed explanation surrounding the sentence passed in this case. I have spoken to Mr Posner the crown advocate in this case, he and the prosecuting barrister discussed the question of whether the sentence imposed was appropriate and they both concluded that it was and should not be appealed. I would not wish to go into technicalities of the sentence in a letter, but would prefer to offer you a face to face meeting with Mr Posner and possibly the barrister, should you wish to have a meeting contact the office.

When I read this letter I felt so down, why would they not want to appeal it. I rang the C.P.S office they gave me an appointment for Wednesday 3rd Feb 2010 at 11am. We went to see our local MP, I explained the way I had been treated, and he said he would write to the CPS and the home office on my behalf.

We had a few replies back from government saying your letter is receiving attention. Between all this we were still looking after the children, Richard was still seeing Peter from victim support, I was still going to the bridge for counciling not that I was copeing very well with it.

I was now allowed to be counciled about the attack and yet I was struggling to talk, we talked about the children. We also talked about Richard and how we were fighting for my rights.

My councilor asked about my sister

I replied, "She never rang me,"

"I didnt get to say goodbye," My councilor said "how sad for you Helen,"

I replied, "I just hope she settles aboard, I wish her all the luck."

"I'm just sad I didn't get to say goodbye."

I also told her I had a letter from probation victim liason officer.

The next few days, were hard we were still living on next to nothing, god I felt so low in myself, poor Richard he looked really tired.

Wednesday 3rd Feb 2010, We took the children to school and headed straight down to town for our meeting at CPS, when we arrived we had to sit in the waiting area, after about 10 minutes we were called into the meeting.

Richard Posner and Rosie Collins the barrister shook our hand's and told us to take a seat. Richard Posner said how sorry he was to hear that I felt disappointed with the legal system.

Rosie explained Mark Shirley's sentence with us, she asked why I didn't feel happy with the sentence Mark got, I told Rosie I wasn't happy because I firmly believed he would get life with no chance of parole considering his past history and the attack on myself: Rosie said she felt Mark would not come out for a very long time, my husband Richard said but their is a chance that he could come out in 9 years time.

Rosie replied, "Yes

Richard there is always that chance."

Richard Posner asked me, "Why I would of wanted to place an appeal."

I told Richard Posner about how Lisa came to my house on 23rd December 09 and told me Mark had 28 days to appeal his sentence.

I told him how I asked her if I had that right of 28 days to appeal, but she didn't answer me; she just carried on dealing with the camera man. Richard Posner said that he and Rosie looked at the sentence and they both agreed they were happy with what the judge gave Mark, so at the time they didn't feel that they needed to bother me.

Rosie said, "I thought you were happy with the sentence Helen"

"No", I replied I even told the media outside court that justice hadn't been done.

I told Richard Posner that I felt that him and Rosie had taken my appeal rights away and that I would be taking it higher because I felt I should of at least been asked at the time.

I also told him that I thought it was very unfair that the offender gets there appeal rights but the victim doesn't get told there's.

I told him that I would be asking for a face to face meeting with Barry Hughes. I thanked Richard Posner and Rosie Collins for seeing us, God I felt so angry and upset when we came away from the meeting, that evening me and Richard wrote a letter to Barry Hughes asking if we could have a meeting with him.

On the 17th Febuary 2010 Barry Hughes wrote to my MP it was basicaly saying that they had a meeting with me to explain the sentencing.

The letter just gave an outline of the 28 days appeal and how you have to act as soon as possible.

As the weeks went on I got a letter from probation Julie Adams- she's an assistant chief officer, she wrote to me to say that she knew that the victim Liaison officer had been in contact with me and that a meeting had been arranged.

She said I do appreciate that having been through an ordeal of a trial, that the ability for the offender to appeal has served to continue the distress you felt, I can only say that I have every confidence that from now on the liason officer will do all she can whilst working with you to keep you fully informed, as promptly as possible when there are developments in the case.

Julie Adams said she has asked to be kepted updated on my case, after reading this letter I felt I really needed the support of the liason officer.

Over the next few weeks, I just got a letter from the parole board basically explaining that they were sorry to hear of the ordeal that I had been through, but they could not discuss Mark Shirley's case with me.

They would be happy to discuss there procedures but nothing else.

I said to Richard, "this is all just getting me down," what is so special about Mark Shirley every one seem's to just want to shut the door, they all no that the wrongs need to be put right.

Richard replied, "I don't know babe don't get down about it, we will get there I promise."

A few days later I had a phone call from Debs at next link,.

"Hi Helen", she said, "I've got something to ask you," Would you like to have a meeting with Alan Johnson from the home office, he would like to meet you to hear your views, he is supporting victim's,"

"God Deb", I replied, "I don't know what to say why me,"

She said, "You have shown so much courage through the media with your fight for justice we thought you would be the right person to meet him,"

I replied, "thanks Deb yes I would love to meet with him."

The meeting was to be held at the bridge in Bristol where I have my counciling.

A few days later I went to the bridge to meet Alan Johnson, I was feeling really scared, when I got there Deb's was waiting for me, Richard and me were taken into a side room Debs made us a coffee.

Alan Johnson arrived he sat down and thanked me and Richard for coming to see him, we sat and talked to Alan for about an hour, you could see in his face that he was really taken back with what I was telling him.

Alan assured me he would do his upmost best to pass on my letter to a colleague at the ministry of justice; he also said he would pass my letter onto barroness stern

I thanked Alan for offering me his support, he replied, "you're very welcome,"

He thanked us for seeing him and told me he would write to me soon, "Thank you", I replied.

When he left the bridge Debs said.

"Well done Helen."

I replied, "Thank's Debs I only hope that it makes things stronger for other victim's," Debs said, "with what you have just told Alan Im sure it will."

On our way home I said to Richard what did you think of Alan, we both agreed you wouldn't of got a nicer man, Richard said at least he took the time to listen.

I was so pleased that I had managed to give Alan Johnson my view of the legal system as I didn't feel that I was just trying to fight for my own right, I wanted to try and help make changes for other victim's.

The following day was very hard as I went to Wales with Richard to visit Mary's grave; but when I got there we couldn't find it so we asked a groundsman if he could take us to Mary's plot as we had walked around for about an hour and couldn't find it. We gave him the plot number and he took us to the plot area.

The groundsman left us.

I got on my knees and took all the long grass away with Richard's help so at least it looked tidy.

I put Mary's flowers on her grave and told her through my heart I would be back soon, walking away from her grave I felt so sad I kept thinking how she was cruely taken out of the world.

We went into the front office of the crematorium and asked the groundsman if I was allowed to come back and sort the grave out so at least it would look nice for Mary, he replied, "yes by all means do,"

"Thank you", I replied.

A few days later Richard and me went back to Wales, we planted rose bushes and we had brought Mary an angel statue, because we had very little money.

Richard had to engrave the angel himself, the grave looked really pretty when we finished, walking away I felt a little better knowing that she had something from me. I now felt I had something that I shared with Mary which has always stayed private to me.

About a week later from finishing Mary's grave I decided to go on GMTV with Lorraine Kelly, again I managed to tell the nation on live tv how I had been treated and how I was going to continue to fight the justice system not just for myself but for other victims to. Lorraine Kelly was really nice.

Her team from GMTV really did work hard they even managed to get a piece out on the six o'clock news where they had asked members of the public if Life Should Mean Life.

GMTV treated me with a lot of respect they were a great team. I was very pleased with myself for doing this as going out in the public really scared me.

On the 16th March 2010 I had a letter from the home office Alan Johnson it read:

**Home Office**

HOME SECRETARY
www.homeoffice.gov.uk

Mrs Helen Stockford                                            16 MAR 2010

Dear Helen,

I wanted to thank you and your husband for taking the time to meet me
on my recent visit to the Bridge and for sharing with me the horrifying
details of the attack and its aftermath. I was very sorry to hear about your
concerns about how your case was handled and its progress through the
criminal justice system.

I have passed your letter onto my colleagues at the Ministry of Justice who
will respond in full to the issues you raised about sentencing. I have also
passed your letter onto Baroness Stern who, as you know, has just published
her review into how rape complaints are dealt with by public authorities
and the criminal justice system in particular. Although sentencing was
outside the remit of Baroness Stern's review I felt it was important that
she was aware of your experiences. Part of her review was to look at what
support we must make available to all victims of these horrific crimes to
enable them to rebuild their lives.

Supporting victims of sexual violence is something that the Government
takes very seriously. I recently asked Sara Payne to complete a piece of
work for my department which looked at what victims should be able to
expect from the criminal justice system in these dreadful circumstances.
This work informed our Violence Against Women and Girls Strategy (I
enclose copies of both reports) which was published in November of last

year. You will see that Sara's report, like Baroness Stern's independent review, recognises that support for victims is not yet consistent across the country, and there are many improvements that we still need to make. Our Strategy was an important step in setting out how we would like support services such as Sexual Assault Referral Centres and Independent Sexual Violence Advisors to work. It is important that specialist sexual violence services like these are there to provide crucial help and advocacy to victims, while ensuring that the criminal justice system deals quickly and robustly with bringing the perpetrators of such crimes to justice.

You also raised with me the importance of providing support to the families and loved ones of victims of sexual offences. This is an area in which we recognise we need to do more, and both SARCs and ISVAs are crucial to our efforts to make this support available. It is also something that we are considering carefully as we take forward the development of the National Victims' Service and in responding to Baroness Stern's recommendations, recognising that these crimes have a much wider impact than just the victim themselves.

My thanks again for meeting with me in Bristol. I appreciate that this must have taken considerable courage on your part, and my very best wishes to you and your family for the future.

Yours sincerely
Alan Johnson

I thought it was really nice of Alan Johnson to take the time and write back to me, he also sent a copy of Sarha Paine's report. The following day I went and seen My Councilor at the bridge in Bristol we spoke about the same things really.

I still couldn't bring myself to talk about the attack and Mary; we did talk about my constant washing and srubbing my self all the time.

My Councilor showed me how to breathe as I kept having panic attacks at home mainly in the bathroom. I told Michelle how I kept getting flash backs of the day of the attack, but they were very quick flashes of the bathroom.

I told Michelle that Liz from CID was coming on the 19th March to hand me over to the victim liason worker from probation, Michelle and me agreed to see each other next week. On the 19th March 2010 Liz from CID called to my house.

"Hi Helen how's things?"

"Not Good". I responded.

I replied, Richard let the liason officer in she introduced herself.

"Hi Im Sarah Smith", she then took a seat in my living room; she started to tell me what her role was.

I couldn't really believe what she was telling me, and I was really taken back by the way she was acting, honestly she was so full of her self her arms were flying around as she was talking.

She then said, "Any questions Helen"

I replied, "Yes can you please slow down and start again as I haven't taken in what your role is".

She looked at me and said I haven't had a victim tell me that before, she started to tell me and Richard that Mark was a cat A prisoner and that he would have to do some courses to work his way down the catagory's to an open prison.

I asked her if Mark Shirley had been moved from Horfield prison Bristol as that was only up the road from where I lived, she said, "I can't tell you what prison he's at but yes he had been moved from Horfield."

I then asked her what sort of courses he would have to take. She said she could not tell me! But she believed he had completed a few already. She then went on to say that I wasn't aloud to contact her in the future, but she would contact me around the parole in the later future, where she would then help me to put a statement in front of the parole board. Liz was looking very confussed and I really didn't no what to think!!

I told her that Julie Adams's letter said that the liason officer was there to support through out the sentence, but Sarah Smith said I have just explained my role to you, she spoke to me in a very rude manner.

She made it very clear that she couldn't discuss Mark's past history with me, I told her I wasn't very happy with the way she had come into my home.

I told her very politley that I thought she was very rude, and told her I was going to speak with Julie Adams. She replied Im sorry you feel that way and left my house.

The following day, I did give Sarah Smith a call to ask a very small question, and God she was very rude.

She replied, "I told you not to contact me I would contact you in the future" I rang probation to request a meeting with Julie Adams.

I explained why we wanted a meeting with her; I think me and Richard both felt let down as we were hoping that the liason officer as promised was going to give us some support.

The days and the weeks just seemed to get harder especially when you're trying to get the family back to normal.

Julie Adams agreed to see us at her office in Bristol, when we got there we were called through to her office.

"Hi Mrs Stockford, Mr Stockford how nice to meet you," we all sat down.

Julie said, "I hope you dont mind but I thought it would be good to have the liason officer at this meeting to see if we can put things right."

The liason officer (Sarah Smith) said, "sorry for the way she came across in my home," she went on to tell me that because there were few liason officers but hundred's of victims there was not enough staff to cover everyone.

She said, "she had at least a couple of hundred victims on her books alone,"

"So that is why", she said she told me not to contact her but she would contact me in the distant future.

I turned to Julie Adams and said, "My god there does need to be changes made as victims are suffering."

She replied, "I agree with you Helen but there just isn't enough resources."

Julie Adams agreed that there were two pathsways for this case, the liason officer for the future parts, but she advised me that she couldn't discuss Mark's past history.

She agreed mistakes have been made but told me to go straight to the top person with my complaints, she gave me Michael Spurr as the top person as she didn't feel it would be fair to start at the bottom and work our way up waisting time, we thanked Julie Adams.

On leaving the meeting we had to pick our children up from school, after school the evening seemed to go with such a rush I thought my poor children I just dont seem to have much time for them like I used to.

We used to, we always seem to be sorting paperwork out (i.e.) letters or meetings, when is it going to end. Over the next few days we wrote to Micheal Spurr, we included a list of mistakes that had been made through probation and parole.

Over the next few months, it was just letters being sent from ourselves to government, probation and parole. We had alot of replys back from ministry of justice a few letters from them saying unacceptable delays in responding which was due to unforseen difficulty in accessing information from prison about Mark Shirley, so many letters from ministry of justice throughout the month's but nothing positive from them.

It was like they were all saying the same thing and they were basically going over themselves, parole seemed to be doing the same thing, no one wanted to give me any answers to why my appeal rights had been taken away no one wanted to answer all the past mistakes (i.e.) the handling of Mark Shirley through probation and parole.

We had a meeting with Barry Hughes which again I felt was a waste of time as he said the time limit had passed for an appeal so there was nothing he could do, he did give me his word that he would try and make victim's better aware of appeal rights and he did say he would correspond with the attorney general Dominic Greeves.

With nothing positive from anyone, life for myself just felt empty, Richard was still seeing Peter from victim support. Family life was not getting any better we were still trying to sell the house as I just didn't feel comfortable in it, Richard had got himself a job, but hand's up I didnt cope home alone so it only lasted a couple of days, as the house and where we lived terrifies me.

I was still struggling with Michelle my councilor it just seemed to get harder and harder I could not express how I felt about the attack, and I could not bring myself to talk about Mary, will I ever find closure with Mary.

Michelle agreed that she was struggling, we both felt that I should of been allowed to talk about the attack from the start but I couldn't as CID had to keep me pure for the court case.

One particular day, as I was cleaning my living room, as I was cleaning a news piece came on the t.v about the James Bulger killer.

James Bulger's mother was on the news with her solicitor; she was basically fighting against what Im trying to fight for (ie) That little boy's killer had been released from prison through parole, given a completely new identity to re-offend again.

I just stopped cleaning and thought to myself where is the justice in this country, why arn't these ministers doing anything right for victims. The offenders get everything, all the rights go to them they are well protected untill they re-offend again and yet it's the public and the victims that have to suffer.

Richard and me decided enough is enough, Richard searched on line to find the solicitor. Eventually found him, the following day Richard rang his office, we were given his email address so that we could send him an email: saying

**Fao Solicitor**

My name is Helen Stockford and I live in Bristol, I am a victim of Mark Shirley a life lience murderer who killed a 67 yr old lady called Mary Wainwright in 1987, he subjected me to a 5hr ordeal in my home in March 2009.

He was given 6 life sentences with a 9 yr tarriff I have had loads of media coverage over the last 8 mths and have tried to get a solicitor that will act on my behalf as my rights were taken away from me because cps failed to tell me about the 28 days appeal.

I had a meeting with Barry Hughes and Richard Posner a few months ago and they addmitted they had failed to tell me about the 28 days but their was nothing he could do for me but he would go and see the attorney general about the 28 days rights & and head of CID to let others who dont get told this at the end of the court case the justice system is wrong.

I am looking to fight for an appeal on the grounds that I was not told of the lenient sentence he got and all so a public enquiry on the handling of Mark Shirleys case and passed history as he should of been given a life determinate sentence with no parole.

He broke all his conditions of his life license as when he was released in 2003.

He had several relationships where probation were not involved and where he did not have to disclose his partners his past history, work placements where he had lots of disaplinarys and eventualy sacked for being drunk at work and being really nasty to women workers and also he was recalled for drink driving and having a sharp implement on him which were part of his life lience conditions and that he should not of done any of these things in 2007 he spent 2 yrs in side and then their was a fiance that told lies in 2008 on a parole hearing regarding the sharp implement which lead to his release due to the cover up of the sharp implement and then in March 2009 he attacked me with 7 life liences now and the judges views that he is a very evil dangerous man that should never be released but had to go by the guide lines of the law.

I am hoping you can represent me for my rights I am willing to travel to Liverpool to see you thank you

Helen Stockford

Dear Mrs Stockford,

I am currently away from my office and have been forwarded your email (set out below).

I have the greatest sympathy for your situation and would, of course, like to assist. However, I do not have any available time – at least for the next few weeks.

Even if I do have time available in the future there are some practical issues to consider including:

(1) Whether anything will be achieved in the sense of you securing something that you wish to happen (other than exploring and pursuing every avenue).

(2) Funding the time and expense involved in dealing with the very difficult and distressing issues: unfortunately, some charge would have to be made for me/my firm providing professional services to you and a suitable funding arrangement would have to be entered into.

[I do not know what your financial circumstances are (you ought to have received compensation for the criminal injuries you suffered: did you have legal advice in pursuing such a claim and have the lawyers assisting in that claim been able to help you more generally?) and there may be others who are prepared to assist in meeting costs. Even if you were financially eligible for funding from the LSC it would not, at present, be possible for my firm to help you as funding is rationed and my firm does not have any available 'matter starts' to take on new matters such as your case]

(3) Approaching your MP to help (if you have not already done so). This may involve pursuing complaints under the *Code of Practice for Victims of Crime:* if you have already exhausted the service provider procedures (against the CPS) – the MP can refer matters to the Parliamentary Ombudsman. The MP may help in seeing whether assistance can be given to secure what you seek requiring independent legal advice about and, if possible, to pursue profound concerns [In *Rebuilding Lives supporting victims of crime* (Cm

6705) published in December 2005 the Government indicated that it wanted "to provide a comprehensive range of support services for victims that are immediate, practical, local and tailored to their needs" but this has not been, I regret to say and as you know something that currently exists].

Yours sincerely

Once we received this email reply, we rang our new M.P. Charlotte Leslie; we explained on the phone to her P.A. that we needed a meeting as soon as possible. Richard did explain why, The P.A was very nice she said she would talk to Charlotte as soon as possible.

Charlotte Leslie gave me an appointment for the 6th August 2010, I managed to prepare a complete file of letters to take with me for Charlotte to look at. When we went to the appointment I showed her all the documents from government, probation and parole, I explained how I'd been treated right from the start of the case!

I explained that I was getting really tired trying to fight on my own just with Richard's support, I told her that I had tried every solicitor around Bristol, Wales, Bath and London but they dont deal with rape cases like mine, "gosh", she replied, so I said to Charlotte that I managed to find a solicitor that might be able to help me if I can get parlimaentary fundings, "so that is why I have come to you", I said, I showed her the emails from the solicitor.

Charlotte said she was going to help me as much as possible, as she felt it was a complete miscarriage of justice, I could feel myself filling up with tears, thank you I replied. Helen I will start work on your case straight away, thank you Charlotte.

When we left her office driving back home with Richard I felt like I was on cloud nine, at last someone has agreed this case is terribly wrong, it felt nice knowing that someone was prepared to help me fight for justice.

The following day I recieved a lovely letter from Charlotte Leslie and I couldn't believe what I was reading, she had sent me a copy of a letter she had sent to the attorney general, I can honestly say I sat and cried because she had done something for me, and the speed of her letter, I could not believe the warmth I felt inside because someone at long last was prepared to help us, Charlottes letter read:

# CHARLOTTE LESLIE MP

CHARLOTTE LESLIE MP

HOUSE OF COMMONS
LONDON SW1A 0AA

## HOUSE OF COMMONS

Mr & Mrs Stockford

6th August 2010

Dear Mr & Mrs Stockford

It was a great pleasure to meet you today, although of course, I wish very much that such a meeting would not have been necessary.

As I said as you left, I will do everything I can to help you. The case you presented struck me as absolutely appalling.

I have written today to the Attorney General, and have enclosed a copy for you below. I will let you know as soon as we have a date and then I will send on more detailed information, and specific requests for the Attorney General.

Once again, can I also say how impressed I was with your professionalism and bravery in the face of the ordeal you have suffered.

Very best wishes,


Charlotte Leslie MP

***Member of Parliament for Bristol North West***

The Rt Hon Dominic Grieve QC MP
Attorney General
Attorney General's Office
20 Victoria Street
London SW1H 0NF

6<sup>th</sup> August 2010

Mrs & Mrs Stockford,

I am writing to request a meeting with you, together with two of my constituents who have suffered an appalling miscarriage of justice.

You may be aware of the case of Helen Stockford, who was raped in her home by local man, Mark Shirley. Helen and her husband Richard have presented me with evidence of proceedings following the attack, which has demonstrated serious flaws in the legal system, which have left the Stockford family, in their words, doubly victimised – by first the attack, and then the System.

I am therefore writing to request a meeting with you, with my two constituents, both to demonstrate these serious flaws in order that these two hard working, brave individuals might see justice, and also in order to inform policy and process going forward.

The Government has given its pledge that it will honour the human rights of victims over those of criminals, and understanding the ordeal that Mr. and Mrs. Stockford have been through in seeking justice will be invaluable in ensuring that the Government presides over a legal system that enshrines the welfare of victims, not criminals.

I understand that your diary will be very busy, but I would not be writing such a letter if the case, and implications of this case, were not very significant indeed.

Thank you in advance,
Best wishes,


Charlotte Leslie MP

Over the month's Charlotte Leslie has give me and Richard very strong support with government, she is also helping Richard with his compensation. In December 2010 she sat in front of the compensation board with Richard, she had given a very strong view to this meeting because even thou she sat with Richard at the panel, they still turned Richard's loss of earnings down on the view that he was home five minutes outside the aftermass time limit to the attack, Charlotte and Richard are still fighting against this they have now asked for a review. The attorney general corresponded with Barry Hughes but there is nothing the attorney general can do to change the fact that I was out of the time limit to appeal. With Charlotte Leslie's help the attorney general agreed I could go to parliment for a meeting with him, the meeting was to be held on January 13ᵗʰ 2011. A full agenda was sent to me prior to the meeting. The agenda read: dated 21ˢᵗ December 2010.

1. Guidance for victims about the sentencing procedure measures to ensure the victim is fully briefed and prepared for all possible sentencing outcomes.
2. Measures to ensure the victim is given time to think about their responce to press outside court (ie beyond guilty/not guilty).
3. Measures to honour the rights of victim's to full information about appealing against the sentence, including-role of C.P.S.- role of the attorney general.


1. Counselling for victims
2. Ensuring that all victims have access to councilling- including those who have been forbidden from talking about the case.
3. Ensuring that claims for compensation are not jeopardised by complications in accessing councilling (as above).


When this agenda came through I could not believe that the attorney general was now willing to see me to discuss all the issues. I was very gratefull to Charlotte, she had worked very hard on my behalf over the months, it had been alot of hard work for me too as I had to prepare paperwork to guide Charlotte so she could then work on it so as to send her views to all the right places. As for us as a family we were still sat with nothing, still sat in the same house as we hadn't sold it. My counselling had been put on hold as Michelle and me were struggling with the fact that I have closed down mentally on the attack, we agreed that yes there are two parts we need to deal with, one trying to put closure on Mary! Can't do that as I dont have a picture to put to the name/two, to come to terms with the fact that I am a victim of Mark Shirley's.

I kept thinking about Christmas, I was so worried because they turned Richard's compensation down, Cathy knew how worried I was she said, "Helen let me help you," I replied, "I can't let you do that," "yes you can", she said, "put Christmas on my credit card," "don't be silly Cathy," I said "I can't do that," she replied, "look thats the least I can do with the mess your in," I agreed I thanked Cathy I thought it was a really kind offer from Cathy, I know we have had our ups and downs but she has tried hard to help where she can and at least we have managed to stay friends for the sake of the children.

We met with the Attorney General on 13th January 2011, Charlotte met us at the house of commons, we sat and had a coffee as we had to go through the paperwork ready for the meeting. We then walked across to the Attorney Generals office, when we arrived the Attorney General introduced us to a member of private office along with Jenny Portway and Nazal from the crown prosecution services, they all said hello and shook our hand's. The Attorney General told me to take a seat and make myself comfortable. He came across as a really nice person. Mrs Stockford he said can I offer you a cup of tea, once he had made the tea

For everyone he came and sat in his chair which was not far from mine, he started the meeting with saying how sorry he felt that it has taken a long time to sort things through before seeing me, I replied, "that's fine."

He asked me to explain what I felt had gone wrong, I started to tell him about the way I had been treated from the sentence, I discussed all the compensation issues with him, we talked about all the mistakes through probation and parole (i.e.) The lies and the statements that had been made by Cathy Smith which helped in Mark Shirley's release. We discussed the handling of Mark Shirley through probation, we talked at great length about my counseling and how I had to stay pure for the court case, and how I'm struggling now with the counseling.

I told him how CID said they would help me by giving me a photo of Mary Wainwright so that I could put a face to Mary's name so that I could try and get some closure, without keep picturing Mary covered in blood, We also spoke about the role of C.P.S. Charlotte Leslie spoke to him about the impact all this has had on our family, she spoke of how we nearly lost our house because of the mortgage, she told him how Richard hadn't gone back to work because his wife needs are to great at the moment. She also discussed Richard's compensation. Ive got to be honest the Attorney General really sat and listened to everything on the agenda and more, the Attorney General said he would write to Louise Casey at the victims commissioner to express his concerns. He also agreed to write to the lord chancellor to raise my concerns regarding both the parole decision and the criminal injuries compensation scheme.

He also commited to write to the home secretary to raise my concerns regarding the police. He said how sorry he felt that the justice system had failed me, he gave me his word that he would do his upmost best to try and help. He thanked me and shook my hand and said he would get started with the letters as soon as possible. I replied, "thank you so much for seeing us," he replied, "your very welcome." After the meeting Charlotte me and Richard could not believe how the Attorney General had gone over the agenda and dealt with a lot more, I told Charlotte, "I thought he was a very nice understanding person." We laughted together as Charlotte said, "not many people get to have a cup of tea made for them by the Attorney General," I replied, "he really did make me feel welcome."

When we got back home I told the children how well the meeting went, I told them that it was looking positive, they were really pleased. My daughter Amy did laugh she said hey mum you can now say you and dad had a cup of tea made by the Attorney General. On the 8th Febuary 2011 I had a knock on my front door, it was a man from the sun news paper, he had come to discuss Mark Shirley!! I told him I could not talk on the doorstep he would have to come in, I mainly asked him in because when he said he had come about Mark Shirley, I felt very unsteady on my feet. He came in and sat down, Richard was at the local shops with my eldest daughter Amy and my little boy Sam, my other daughter Molly I sent her into Cathy's house next door.

The man from the sun news paper said that Mark Shirley had got himself a pen-pal which he had been writing to for sometime from his prison cell, he said that the pen-pal had sold all the letters to the sun paper. He said the letters intailed a lot of pornography, he said that Shirley had fantasized about what hed like to do to a woman in a dangerous manner, I felt sick to my stomach, I asked the man if I had been mentioned me in the letters, he said, "lets just say most of the letters are to disscusting to print, but because you are a victim of Shirley's we wanted to let you know because they are going in Thursdays paper." He asked me if I was ok, I replied, "not really how has he managed to do this he is supposed to be a catergory A prisoner who gets everything checked," he said, "no he's not a cat A prisoner," I asked the man what he ment, he said he's a catergory B prisoner, he told me he had always been a cat b prisoner even when he murdered Mary Wainwright. By this point I felt really ill, I replied, "are you sure," he replied, "yes," he told me I could view the letters if I wanted to but I would have to travel down to London, he would get someone to meet me, I told him I was due in London tomorrow 9th Febuary to see the victim commissioners, he said he would get someone to meet with me after the meeting. I heard my husband and the children pulled up outside, sorry I told him you will have to leave, I dont want my children to know and get upset, he was very nice, I told the children he was the gas man, Richard guessed different.

Over night I felt so ill, as Richard he was really angry that he had managed to re-offend from prison, we felt very let downby the system. The following day we traveled down to London for the meeting with Louise Casey.

We had to meet Charlotte Leslie at the house of common's, we went through the security check to meet Charlotte in the building, when we met Charlotte I told her that the sun news paper had come out to my home to warn me that Mark Shirley had a pen-pal had sold the letters to the sun, "O my goodness", she replied, I told her that I had been told that Mark Shirley had fantasized through the letters and they were full of pornography, I told her that the sun were willing to meet me after todays meeting to show me the letters.

Charlotte asked me, "when it was coming out in the news paper," I replied, "tomorrow the 10th Febuary 2011 now." Charlotte moved very quickly she rang several different departments to see what could be done to stop the piece going to print, the media complaints commisioners could not stop it from going to print either but they did tell them I didnt want to comment on what had happened as they were going to use the conversation from my home.

Charlotte took me and Richard across to the minisry of justice building where we met Louise Casey. On meeting with Louise Casey we had discussed a lot of different issues surrounding my case, she also had a very strong letter from the attorney general.

Even thou she can't interveen in individual cases Louise assured me she would continue to liase with the attorney general on my case.

A lot of my experiences and views can hopefully make a valuable contribution to informing her work on improving services and support for future victims, Louise Casey also gave me alot of guidance on different areas in my case that I still need to persue. On meeting Louise Casey I found her to be a very understanding person that definately feels and works very hard for victims, you can definately see that she takes her role seriously, and Im very sure that as time goes on I will get to meet her again.

I also told Louise that if there is anyway I can help towards making changes or to voice some of my experiences then I would do so, as I really feel strong about making changes for other victims.

Richard and Charlotte walked out of the room and Louise Casey took me back in the room, I thanked Louise for seeing me, she shook my hand and hugged me and she said you look after yourself and dont get down over whats comming out in the sun paper.

When we came away from the meeting I thanked Charlotte, I decided not to meet with the sun news paper to read the letters from Mark Shirley to the pen-pal. I just didnt want to come face to face with the dirt that was in them.

Charlotte continued to rattle the ministers, Richard spoke with probation service (Julie Adams) she told Richard she hadn't heard anything about the letter so she would have to look into it. Charlotte said, "that government are very sympathetic Helen," I thanked Charlotte for all her hardwork, we agreed we would talk later or tomorrow.

Richard and myself headed back home to Bristol, I felt so emotionaly upset inside, it felt like Shirley had the upper hand again, throughout the night I just sat and thought how much more is Shirley going to be allowed to do, why arn't the prison services stopping him. The following morning Richard took our little boy to school.

I decided to keep my teenage girls home for the day as I didnt want anyone at school to make a comment if they were to read it (via) the paper or internet.

My husband did buy the news paper so we could see what had been said, for me as a victim I could read between the lines of the sick letters printed, which were full of sick fantasies, welcome to Shirly's sick world I thought to myself and this is a sick man that eventually in years to come will be eligible for parole, they also printed that Mark Shirley was still in Horfield prison which is still down the road from me even thou Sarah Smith assured us he had been moved.

Charlotte phoned me to say she was still working hard, I told Charlotte I wanted to see the Attorney General, home secretary, and others; we decided to fight for a full review. Charlotte told me it could take some time as ministers are busy people, I told Charlotte I didnt care how long it takes.

As time has gone on I have been told by Charlotte that the ministers are liasing about the review, I have also had a letter back from the attorney general following the meeting we had.

Its a very positive letter and yes he has done everything he said he would do, obvouisly its going to take him sometime with the other minister's which I can fully understand, but part of his letter read: At the meeting with the Attorney General, the C.P.S officials present mentioned that their working on revising the C.P.S victims and witness's policy.

Victim and witness care is a core part of the role of the cps, but admittedly the layering of commitments and initiative's has created a complex framework and made it difficult for victims and witnesses to know what they should expect and from whom. The cps is working to simplify their commitments to ensure efforts are targeted to give the right level of support based on the level of need. I can assure you that the points you have raised Helen have been fed into that work. Improved cps process and procedures should be in place for 2012, although any changes that require legislation may be implemented later. I was so overwhelmed when I read this letter, as in my heart I knew that I had managed to make changes for other victims which would be in place in 2012.

I was so pleased Richard gave me a hug he looked so pleased for me, we both agreed that it makes you feel that this journey we are both on is worthwhile, especially if it's going to help changes for other victims. I know in my heart that I still have a very long journey in front of me while I wait for minister's to reply.

**I'd press my hand against your
throat. You would feel abused
when we are done**

PRINT

**Sun**

FEATURES·

EXCLUSIVE

# I'd press my hand against your throat. You would feel abused when we are done

**Evil... cold-eyed killer Mark Shirley**

A VICIOUS murderer and rapist is acting out sick sex attack fantasies in letters to a female pen pal from his prison cell.

In one of the most shocking crimes of the past ten years, knife-wielding monster Mark Shirley repeatedly raped mum-of-five Helen Stockford.

At the time he was on parole from a life sentence for killing 67-year-old widow Mary Wainwright in 1987.

During Helen's horrific ordeal in March 2009, Shirley related details to her of his attack on Mary.

He was again jailed for life in December 2009 and told he would serve at least nine years before being considered for release.

*But today The Sun can reveal Shirley has described graphic scenes of abuse in a series of letters –– despite the fact prison authorities are allowed to censor mail.*

Scandal

The letters –– which contain chilling echoes of his crimes –– went out to a woman over a five-month period.

**Courageous... victim Helen Stockford**

Last night there were demands from a former top cop for an inquiry into the scandal.

It came to light as Shirley plans his appeal against conviction for the attack on 41-year-old Helen, who has bravely waived her right to anonymity.

Amazingly only prisoners inside Category A and high-security prisons **MUST** have mail vetted. In Category B jails, like the one holding Shirley, governors have the power to open mail if they think it could cause distress or anxiety to the person receiving it.

This loophole meant the killer was apparently free to indulge fantasies of rape and aggression in writing.

*In his string of lurid letters to a female pen pal, Shirley:*

Tells how he dreams of stalking victims before pouncing on them in their homes.

Creates elaborate scenarios to fulfil his cravings for the act of rape.

Writes of drug and alcohol abuse in his Category B prison.

Vows to get his conviction quashed.

In one note from last July, littered with spelling errors — as are all his scrawls — Shirley describes how he might ensnare a victim. A chilling segment of it appears on this page.

Chilling

It continues: "I push you up against the wall hard and press my hand against your throat... you would feel very used and abused when we are done."

In another note, part of which is also pictured, he writes: "I tell you to shut up... you cry out and I tell you to shut up and take it."

At the time of Shirley's conviction, Mrs Stockford said: "I do not feel justice has been done. I want him locked up for life with no chance of parole. I want to know how this man managed to come out on parole. My family and I need those answers."

**Sick... killer's note to female pen pal**

The results of a Parole Board Review Committee probe on that issue have yet to be announced.

*No one was more surprised than Shirley that he was allowed to get away with communicating his sick fantasies while inside jail.*

He said in another note to the pen pal: "I'm glad you finally got my letter I was not sure if they stopped it going out because our mail gets censored."

## Maimed

Shirley –– Prisoner A1388AP –– also tells how he hopes to have his rape conviction overturned. He wrote: "As for a solicitor I have found one who is willing to look into my case.

"It could take a few year's. All I can do is stay positive and hope."

*In further letters Shirley criticises the jail culture of booze and drugs.*

He said: "This place was pretty loud and noisy over Christmas and especially at new year –– most people were drugged up or drunk. There's plenty of both in these places." In 1987, aged 16, Shirley stalked Mary for weeks before torturing and murdering her in her Cardiff home.

She was maimed with knives and choked on her own blood. Shirley left an ornamental knife and a 2p coin as "gifts" on her stomach.

Released on parole after serving 16 years, he began a relationship with a neighbour of Mrs Stockford in Southmead, Bristol.

When the relationship ended –– Shirley having been recalled to jail for drink-related offences but subsequently released –– he focused his evil intent on Mrs Stockford.

*And in March 2009 he struck, imprisoning her at her home.*

It was a Friday morning and the married mum had been cleaning upstairs. She came downstairs to find Shirley had broken in and was sitting at her kitchen table.

He produced a bag full of knives and forced her to sit on a chair.

Giving evidence at his trial, where he denied the attack, Mrs Stockford said: "He then began making howling noises and ordered me to lie on the table. He took my black top off and then he flicked his knife open.

undress And take all my cloths of And wait
for you to come out of the Bathroom finally
you come out with A towell Around you And
walk into your Bedroom I grab you By your
hair And you yell out I tell you to shut
up And do what I tell you I turn Round while
holding your hair And kick the Door shut with
my leg then I push you onto your knees

## 'I push you onto your knees'... rapist's fantasy was allowed through in prison mail

"I did think, 'Oh my God, I am not going to get out of here'.

"He then said he once knew a lady, a sweet lady, her name was Mary. He said that he had watched her for a long time.

"He said I was sweet like her. He said he stamped around in her blood.

"That's when he told me that he had defaced her. He seemed to be laughing to himself."

### Controlled

Describing him as "cold-eyed", she went on: "He said that Fridays and Saturdays were good drinking and killing days."

Shirley then raped Mrs Stockford four times over three and a half hours. Her ordeal was only ended when her 19-year-old son called at the house, forcing Shirley to abandon the attack.

While Shirley still shows contempt for his victims and their families, he bleated in his letters: "(At Christmas) I kept myself busy and worked all the way through it so it took my mind off the fact I was in here and could not be with the people I cared about. The people here are selfish and only care about themselves and not about their families or children or what they put them through by being in here."

*And Shirley may soon be getting new cellmates to complain about.*

He has undergone psychological evaluation and tells his pen pal: "I'm waiting for them to write there final report. I believe as soon as that is done they will make a final decision on what prison I will be moved to."

A Prison Service spokesman told The Sun last night: "Prisoners' communications are controlled to protect the public from unwanted or unlawful contact.

"We are looking into this case to prevent it from happening again."

n.francis@the-sun.co.uk

**myView**
by JOHN O'CONNOR

THESE letters should result in Shirley having days knocked off his remission. All material sent out of prison should be monitored.

These guys are serving a term of imprisonment and part of that should be that they cannot send salacious, threatening or abusive material from behind bars.

The Prison Service has the tools to deal with this and must make sure they do.

It's not good enough that this sort of material is being allowed out from a man like Mark Shirley.

Murderer acts out sick sex attack fantasies in letters to a female pen pal from his priso...

Maybe there is a mistaken view they would be breaking human rights legislation by censoring mail but they should still be ensuring people are protected from those behind bars.

It's shocking this is being allowed to happen and it's right that this man should be exposed for it.

I hope action will now be taken to ensure he is not allowed to continue this.

# WAITING FOR A MEETING WITH THE MINISTRY OF JUSTICE

As the hard weeks and month's passed it felt like every day got longer every few weeks I would text poor Charlotte Leslie my MP always saying the same thing is there any news on my meeting with Ken Clarke yet i.e.: the minister of justice, she would say not yet you know ministers take their time sorry! AS time passed I did a radio four piece in support of the work Louise Casey was doing for bereaved families and victims.

The radio four show was called A VOICE FOR VICTIMS this was good for me as I felt I was doing something to help others, plus it felt good because at least I was able to tell people how one day of crime changes a victim's life and how and what effects it has on the victim's family. After long months of battling and preparing paperwork, Crispin Blunt sent me a letter dated 9th May 2011, saying thank you for your email of 3rd May 2011 in which you asked for an update to our letter of 18th February 2011 to the justice secretary.

Firstly may I say again how sorry I am that you feel so let down by the criminal justice system, following the appelling offence committed against you by Mark Shirley? I assure you that I take your concerns very seriously indeed and I have asked my officials to look into the issues you raised thoroughly. As you know Charlotte Leslie has been in touch with me about your case and I offered to meet her to discuss the issues raised. I'm pleased to say that I will be meeting Charlotte on the 18th May 2011.

I'm afraid I cannot meet you at this time but following the meeting with Charlotte I will write again to you to let you know the outcome and will also provide you with a full response to the point raised in your February letter from Crispin Blunt. On reading this letter I got very upset and cross as I first wrote to Ken Clarke with all the points I wanted to raise with Charlotte's help.

This letter made me feel like Ken Clarke couldn't be bothered so he just handed it to Crispin Blunt to deal with. A few days later I met with Charlotte and told her my views she agreed with me and said it would be more beneficial to have me in a meeting so we could both go through the agenda. She agreed to cancel this meeting of the 18th May 2011 and battle again to see if he would agree to meet with us both. As time passed every day week and month seemed to get longer and longer, I watched as Ken Clarke made a real blunder with a rape victim on TV which really made me upset and very cross, at the time the media did contact me but Charlotte told me it was best not to get involved as I needed to stay polite as she advised me that I had to stay on the right side of the ministers because of the meeting so as upset as I felt for all the rape victims I couldn't do anything to support them which was very hard for me.

The Rt Hon Kenneth Clarke QC MP
Secretary of State for Justice
Ministry of Justice
102 Petty France
London SW1H 9AJ

18th February 2011

Dear Mr Clarke

Ref: Helen and Richard Stockford,

I am writing to request a meeting with you, together with my MP, Charlotte Leslie, to discuss aspects my case that comes under the remit of your department.

You may be aware of my case: I was raped in my home by a local man, Mark Shirley. My husband Richard and I have presented our MP with evidence of proceedings both before and after the attack, which has demonstrated serious flaws in the justice system, which have left us feeling doubly victimised – by first the attack, and then the System.

We have already met with both the Attorney General and the Victims Commissioner and would now like the opportunity to discuss failings that our case has highlighted that fall under the Ministry of Justice's remit, in order that we might see justice, and also in order to inform policy and process going forward, with Charlotte Leslie's help.

I know the Government has given its pledge that it will honour the human rights of victims over those of criminals, and understanding our ordeal in seeking justice may help in ensuring that the Government presides over a justice system that enshrines the welfare of victims, not criminals.

The summer months were very long for my children especially the summer holidays as with not much money we could not afford a family holiday or any day trips, it was very stressful as we had people viewing the house with no luck in selling it. It was very stressful as the bills were just rising, we got supporting letters from the GP and MP to try and keep the company's at bay finally the children went back to school.

On the 6ᵗʰ October 2011 at long last I received a letter from Crispin Blunt it read; Thank you for your letter of the 7ᵗʰ September 2011 accepting my invitation to meet you together with your constituent Helen Stockford. The comprehensive summary of the issues which you wish to discuss with me and which you set out in your letter is extremely helpful and will help to structure the meeting. I should explain however as I am sure you will understand, that I am not the best placed to discuss some of the issues which you raise as these are more appropriately directed to the crown prosecution service.

These include why Mrs. Stockford was not informed of the time limit on her right to appeal Mark Shirley's sentence and why Mr. & Mrs. Stockford were not better prepared for various sentencing outcomes, my office will be in contact with MP Charlotte Leslie to arrange a mutually convenient time to meet.

There was part of me that felt very pleased at long last he's agreed a meeting I thought! But there also was a part of me that was upset as we were told that the ministry of justice dealt with all justice issues and yet Crispin Blunt was basically saying the crown prosecution service wasn't in there remit.

I spoke with Charlotte and we all agreed to meet on the 31ˢᵗ October 2011, a full agenda was sent to Crispin Blunt, I have placed this agenda in with my story for you all to share and read.

<u>Mrs. Stockford Meeting</u>
Mrs Stockford Agenda

## **Suggested general changes:**

<u>Crown Prosecution Service:</u>
To find a mechanism to enable:

- More guidance for victims about sentencing procedure and options for appeal; particularly regarding the time limit on their right to appeal against a sentence, and the remit of that appeal.
- Victims to have more time to think about their response to the verdict and sentence, particularly when the press is likely to be outside court, and not be dictated to by a media circus.
- Counselling for victims at all stages including in situations where the victim is told not to talk about the case and a procedure in place if the victim has to remain 'pure'.
- Better support, including financial help, for the families of victims – and look at ways of redressing the practical balance of a seeming 'assumption against' the victim to a 'presumption for'.

<u>Probation Service</u>
To find a mechanism to ensure:

- The Probation Service acts swiftly to recall prisoners on license when other offences are committed (Routinely more swiftly than in this particular case.)
- The Parole and Probation Service contextualises evidence provided to it regarding offenders when given by those in a close personal relationship with them.

<u>The Prison Service</u>

- To categorise prisoners based on more information than simply escape risk; taking into account the effect on a victim of having a criminal housed in a prison in their local community, particularly when that criminal is from the local community and has contacts there.

- There should be a statutory requirement that prior to release, murderers and sex offenders take the SOPT Programme (Sex Offender Treatment Programme), it should not be optional.
- To reset the balance of Human Rights back towards the victim In terms of:
- Access to victim's documents by a short-term partner of the offender; and a short-term partner's influence through the offender's sollicitor in terms of statements of support etc at parole to be contextualised less in favour of the offender
- Right of the victim, like the offender, to have a solicitor present at the parole board meetings.
- Legal status of Parole Board Hearings: For evidence given at Parole Board Hearings to be made under oath, so that all statements carry a legal status and misinformation is treated accordingly.

## Case-specific questions
Questions regarding the release of Mark Shirley

- Why was Shirley's denial of killing Mrs Wainwright during his first trial and time in prison not made a factor in his sentence for his next crime?
- Why was he released after being recalled for verbal abuse of his probation officer?
- Why was he not recalled in 2006 when reported for being drunk and in breach of his motorcycle license?
- Why was he not immediately recalled after being arrested in 2007 for drink driving while also in possession of a sharp implement?

Failures of the Probation Service

- Failure to inform Cathy and Linda, Mark's girlfriends, of Mark Shirley's past and his license conditions
- Failure to act on his repeated breaches of license

Failures of the Crown Prosecution Service

- Why was Mrs Stockford not informed of the time limit on her right to appeal Mark Shirley's sentence?
- Why were Mr and Mrs Stockford not made better prepared for various sentencing outcomes – they only had statements prepared for guilt/not guilty – so they were not able to fully express their opinion to the press

## Victims' Commission -Victims' Law recommendations

Several recommendations have already been made by the Victim's Commission regarding bereaved families which are also relevant to this case, and cases such as this. Namely:

- That the police will keep the victim / victim's families updated at each stage of the investigation
- Victims and families have a right to information from the CPS and to meet with the CPS lawyer at key stages of the process, including on conviction, or acquittal and on appeal
- There is a new Criminal Procedure Practice Direction about the needs and treatment of victims and victims' families in court.
- That the family are provided with an integrated package of help and support following the offence and up until any trial and beyond. This should include:
  + A dedicated caseworker providing support and advice on practical problems arising from the offence
  + Access to specialist help on issues like housing and child care proceedings arising as a consequence of the offence.
  + Access to trauma counselling from approved providers to help them through trauma
  + Access to a national network of peer support groups who can provide befriending and support for families.

On the 31st October 2011 as scared as I felt myself and Richard headed down to London for the meeting with Crispin Blunt, our children wished us luck they had little smiles on their faces, it was like they were trying to say hopefully the meeting will go well and life will start getting back to normal I gave each of them a kiss and promised I'd be back in time for Halloween, we met Charlotte in the parliament building and she walked us across to the Ministry Of Justice Building Petty France. Charlotte myself and Richard were invited into the meeting room where Crispin Blunt shook my hand and introduced himself, there were two other's in the meeting Jane Saddon and another person but I was so nervous at the time I can't remember her name as you can all read from the meeting note's which I have added in my story, The meeting was very full with discussions

## HELEN'S MEETING NOTE'S FROM WHAT WAS DISSCUSSED FROM THE AGENDA WITH Crispin Blunt

1. Crispin Blunt said that I was the first victim he has seen and that he does not see victims as he would have about 50,000 victims trying to see him, if media were to get hold of information that he had seen a victim and that we know how the media works with information.

2. He said my case is a high profile case and that is why he decided to see me he also said that a lot of lessons have been learnt by my case and that they have used my case to try and change certain things within the system.
   I asked him about counseling changes for victims as I feel all victims should have someone to talk to on the grounds it is private and confidential like going to the G.P.

3. He said that seeing a doctor isn't always private he said for counseling it would be used by the defence that you could of been trained to use certain things to discus to try and make the case stronger.
   So I said there is still no help in counseling as the defence evidence would go against victims even thou it is supposed to be private and confidential.

4. He mentioned that the life sentence even if they are a danger once they have served their sentence they are free to leave prison and

that they would see a probation officer once a week once a month and then every three months.

5.   He sat opposite me and said he could not look me in the eyes and say he would change the law about probation officers handling of Mark Shirley as he said they have ticked all the boxes so there job had been done and they were right to do so.
I said so they can sit in front of probation drunk and abusive and they still tick there boxes and let them leave the office back into the community.
Crispin Blunt replied that they would of ticked there boxes and that's there job.
I asked if that was for every offender
Crispin Blunt replied yes he went on to say that there prisons are really over full and the government has run out of money.

6.   CPS changes he would not discuss as it was not in his remit.

7.   We spoke of parole board hearings:
I asked him if victims could have the same as the offenders (i.e.) solicitors at parole hearings.
Crispin Blunt replied no as parole hearings are about the offenders and the crime and the progress they have made in prison to come back into the community, the most victims are allowed is a statement which you make through probation liaison workers.
I replied in my case I learned that there were lies told and a statement made by Shirley's girlfriend plus through Shirley's solicitor Mary Wainwrights paperwork was given to the girlfriend to read which was part of my trial, I told him I felt this needed changing as a victim, as I would not want a future girlfriend to read my documents, I also asked if parole hearings could be changed to all witnesses being under oath so mistakes cannot be made specially by short term partners.
Crispin Blunt replied no!

8.   We discussed the postal side of prison because of the pen-pal story that came out in the Sun newspaper 10th Feb 2011.

Crispin Blunt replied all CAT B prisoners get their post checked for the first year but after that year is up it does not get monitored as they don't have enough workers to check the post.

After about an hour the meeting ended, I thanked Crispin Blunt for seeing me as upset and angry as I felt. We went back to Charlotte's office where I discussed my views I think she under stood that I wasn't happy with some of the things discussed in the meeting. She said that it was very hard for Crispin Blunt to meet with a victim we both really didn't know where to go for some sort of justice from this meeting.

Traveling back to Bristol I was very upset and Richard was very angry as well.

I had to explain to my children that the meeting didn't go very well, they were very upset because as a family we were all very much hoping to put an end to everything that we have suffered. I and Richard were thinking of bringing it out in the media to see if I could get some support with justice but I felt to wore out and ill. After a week or so I started to pull myself together I started to text Charlotte to see if there was any update on the meeting,

My first text dated 15.11.11

Hi Charlotte any update from the meeting thanks Helen X

Charlotte text I back saying;

No not yet wouldn't expect anything this soon.

My second text dated 15.11.11

Ok no problem I've sat and gone over the meeting ad I think it was very poor, he's basically saying as long as probation ticked their boxes offenders can do anything, it's not good is it, do you think if you get a moment later you can give me a call please as there's a few strong points I think I'd like to discuss with you thanks Helen x

Charlotte text me back saying;

Hi sorry frantic today but I think he was trying to say the opposite, that in the past ticked boxes meant that no one cared what happened as long as people ticked boxes but they are abolishing the tick box culture so people themselves are answerable for their decisions.

I text Charlotte back saying;

Sure but that still don't help victims like me mistakes were made with the handling of Shirley, but because probation ticked there boxes at the time he agrees they have done their job properly, that's very poor how many more cases like mine Helen x

Charlotte text back saying;

I know trying to think what we can do

I text Charlotte back saying;

That makes two of us lol, are you in Bristol this week if so can we look at points together please as I feel we need both strong heads to fight this as we've got this far Helen x

I didn't here back from Charlotte.

A few weeks past and still know news from Charlotte, we were very busy as Richard had found a buyer for our house, was feeling very stressed.

On the 24th November 2011 Crispin Blunt wrote me a letter which again I have added this is in with my story for you all to read and share, as you can see on reading this letter I felt very pleased that some of the improvements had been made in areas that I have been very much involved in, but I still felt very upset and let down as he didn't take the time to improve any of the mistakes in my case (i.e.) probation or parole.

*Helen Stockford*

Charlotte Leslie MP
House of Commons

28 November 2011

Dear Charlotte,

MR & MRS STOCKFORD REGARDING THE VICTIMS' COMMISSIONER'S REVIEW INTO THE NEEDS OF BEREAVED FAMILIES

Thank you for your letter of 2 November on behalf of your constituents Mr Richard Stockford and Mrs Helen Stockford, following our meeting on 31 October. I would like to take this opportunity to thank Mr and Mrs Stockford for taking the time to speak to me about their experience and recommendations for improving the Criminal Justice System.

I am sorry that we did not have time to cover all of the issues that Mr and Mrs Stockford wanted to raise, in particular the recommendations made in the Victims' Commissioner's review into the needs of bereaved families. The recommendations are contributing to a full review of victims' services and support being conducted by the Ministry of Justice and there will be a full public consultation on our proposals later this year. This will include consideration of how support for victims through the criminal justice process can be improved.

Following the publication of the Commissioner's report, the Justice Secretary agreed an additional £500k to ensure five extra caseworkers for the Homicide Service, additional support for professional counselling, advocacy training for caseworkers and funding for peer support groups.

The Government has also prioritised investment in services for victims of sexual violence. We have placed Rape Support Centres on a secure financial footing, allocating £8.5 million of grant funding to existing centres across the country over the next three years. We are also working with the voluntary sector to develop new rape support centres where there are gaps in provision. We have already allocated a total of £600k to develop four new centres in Dorset, Devon, Hereford and Trafford.

I enclose a copy of this letter for you to send to Mr and Mrs Stockford, should you wish to do so.

CRISPIN BLUNT

# The Terrible Ordeal Of
# Selling Our House

As family things were really hard I felt like the justice system had let me down badley but at this time there was a sense of not knowing what to do.

Richard had found a private developer who wanted to buy our house, we had to get supporting letters from my G.P and MP as the buyer only wanted to pay £86,000 for the property.

After a few weeks ge money our mortgage broker decided because of the ordeal that we had suffered at the property and the length of time it had been on the market, with the stigma that sat with the house they agreed the sale.

Our mortgage sat at £132,000 but GE Money agreed a sum of £86,000 as full and final payment. The sale was completed on the 25th November 2011.

We had a few problems with the buyer before the sale as he was struggling to get the mortgage, the sale of our house was going to leave us homeless with nothing, and I and Richard agreed if the buyer was going to continue with mortgage problems we were going to pull out.

I didn't trust the buyer plus there was a very big part of me that didn't want to sell the house as I didn't feel ready plus I was very scared as we had nothing financially to get another house.

Richard saw things very different from me as he felt Id lived there two years to long in a crime scene it was terrible, we were both very stressed we had lots of arguments.

I had no choice so I started packing the house praying the buyer would just pull out, packing my house after sixteen years of living there was very emotional and hard for me, their were nice memories of my children and family life in the house, but also very mixed emotions of what I went through on that terrible day so my emotions were very up and down.

We went to the council with a lot of supporting letters and told them the situation we were in; they said they couldn't help us until the sale was final as we were still classed as home owners.

I was now feeling very worried and scared but it was hard because for the first time I felt I couldn't talk to Richard and if I tried he would just come back with the same thing if we don't sell it they will just repossess it in a few months' time I really believed Richard thought he was doing the right thing, and we would just clash if we tried to discuss the house.

The sale finally completed on the 25th November 2011, I just felt numb we went back to the council with all our support and a letter of sale, Bristol City council wasn't very helpful the most they would allow us was to register with them and they offered us homeless i.e. 3 bedroom bb which was in a very rough area above a kebab shop, a 3 bedroom house miles across the city which would of meant the children would all have to leave their school, they had been through too much already I thought.

South Gloucestershire council offered us a bb in a farm unit with ten different family's and with what I suffer with on a day to day i.e. post-traumatic stress panic attacks and agoraphobia I just started to feel really ill and very low.

The buyer of our house allowed us to stay at the sum of £ 1,100 but he wanted us to leave by the 5th Jan 2012, both councils told us to try and find private rented accommodation housing benefit paid our rent to the private owner of the house while we stayed there. We were also told by the council's to start bidding on the home choice website.

Bristol council put us at banding A and south Gloucestershire council put us at banding C we started bidding but there wasn't very many houses.

I was feeling very worried and scared as I knew on the 5th Jan 2012 I had to go through my own front door for ever. Richard was starting to look like he knew he had made a mistake.

Richard agreed to put another bathroom in the extension of the property for the new buyer I didn't take the pace of this very well as I felt like my home that I spent sixteen years in with my family was just being changed as the new owner was turning it into bedsits for students I kept thinking you have to be strong (Helen) for the children sake as they were looking very sad this is very hard for them I thought, it was very stressful packing their bedrooms.

Richard was looking at the private rented houses near to the children's school after viewing a couple that we sort of liked trying to raise a deposit was very hard which meant we lost those houses we viewed as housing benefit don't cover deposits. Battling with the council was really getting hard I had a friend in the council she did her upmost to help me.

I've known her for fifteen years and she's a lovely lady she gave me a lot of support, she dealt with all the letter writing for us I wouldn't of achieved the letter without her I felt to wore out. My G.P Karen was very good to me she put me on higher tablets as I was very very low.

Richard found another private house with a ten minute walk from the children's school, we went and viewed it, it was a nice house very small but it was clean and tidy, a family friend lent us the money for the deposit the rented house was agreed, Christmas was very hard as the house was packed up, it was very sad as we all knew it was our last one at our house the mood was very low with the children.

After Christmas the children started back to school we had some shocking news over Christmas which took me back to day one of my attack. Richard ordered a van and started to move our things, deep inside me I felt very sad and hurt as I knew I wasn't ready to leave the home that I once loved.

We got the other house ready for the children to move in to we did the move over a few days so the house would be ready to move into, once the house was straight Richard made contact with the buyer and arranged for him to collect the keys as we had ran over a couple of days.

On the 9th Jan at lunch time as I sat in my empty house feeling very numb the buyer turned up with a partner of his no one spoke to me they all just over looked me as they started bringing in cabinets and measuring the walls and floors with their builder.

I just looked around myself it felt a bit like I was stood in a dream my eldest son said, "come on mum you don't need to be treated like this lets wait in the car" I was very sad and hurt.

I didn't feel like Id had a chance to walk around the house and say my good byes to the good and the bad things it was so horrible, as for Richard he was just talking to the new home owner like he felt nothing for the house that was once our home.

Settling into this private rented house has been really hard, to me it really don't feel like home as I know it's not my house apart from my furniture we can't decorate it or make it feel homely, the shops are too far away so without Richard I can't get there as I don't go out alone.

All the street lights go off at night which terrifies me as I don't know the area at all so life just feels very low at the moment as we are just stuck in the middle of thornbury surrounded by bushes and trees, I have know friends or family in the area the only person I see is my councilor once a week which is very hard as she is helping me come to terms with the fact that I'm not in Shirley's bubble back at the old house, trying to cope with the life skill work with her is very hard, as for the council I'm still bidding on the houses but nothing yet.

I really miss my old house and just wish I could go home I didn't think through one day crime I would lose everything it's a real battle as we have to try and start again but until my health improves its going to be very hard plus I have a new ordeal which I'm going through which is very hard to come to terms with as you will all read as you continue to read my story.

## The Day Cid Came Back Out To My House To Update Me

On December 28th 2011, I received a text message from Liz Coles my previous CID officer to say she needed to come out and update me.

I'm being honest I just froze I text her back to say, "Has Shirley got out of prison?"

She replied, "No."

So I rang her and asked her what the update was she said

"I can't tell you by phone Helen what the update is so we agreed she would come out to me."

She said she was coming out with two other officers from CID we agreed they would call to the house at 10am the following day, the rest of the day went really long I was feeling very stressed and didn't have a clue what Liz was going to be updating on, I was very worried.

I had to explain to Richard which was really hard for me as I couldn't tell him why they were coming I also had to ask my mum if she could have the children in the morning, again this was hard as I had to explain that CID were coming out to see me.

My mother asked me, "why are they coming Helen,"

"I don't know mum" I replied.

It was a very long night as my brain was thinking all sorts of things like would they tell me if Shirley had broken free as the way I have been treated over the couple of years by the system I just didn't trust them.

The following morning I woke my children early, I felt quite sad for them as they left to go to their grandmother's house.

They were looking at me with as much to say, "why are CID coming out to you now mum," I gave them a kiss and said, "don't worry kids mum will be fine I will pick you up as soon as there gone I promise."

At 10am there was a knock at the door, it was Liz, "Hi Helen" Liz said, I replied, "Hi!"

She had another officer with her, she introduced him as Ian Hieron from CID he shook mine and Richard's hand and sat down in my living room, Liz said, "gosh it's been a while Helen how's things"

I replied, "Yeah things are ok in the middle of moving but yea things aren't to bad thanks, anyway Liz why have you come out to me and what's to update," I asked.

Ian then started to talk Helen I need to explain that another victim has come forward, she came forward back in February 2011 when the pen-pal story came out in the sun newspaper. This women Helen didn't take the story to well and went to her G.P, the G.P Helen sent her to the mental health team who then sent things across to us at CID. We have been working with this lady Helen since February 2011.

As Ian was explaining things to me I felt sick to my stomach, I turned to Richard and said.

"See I told you there was more victims," Ian said

"Helen listen her attack was before yours so it's classed as historic."

I replied, "I know Ian."

Ian then asked if I knew anything that might make this ladies case stronger as she doesn't have any DNA or medical evidence to support her case; I asked Ian if Mark Shirley had been charged for this lady.

He replied, "Yes".

Ian then explained how her attack was similar to mine, Ian then explained the other reason he had come out to me, it was to tell me I couldn't do anymore media or government work. He served me with a piece of paper which state's they would prosecute me if I were to do anymore work pending this ladies trial, as they didn't want it jeopardize in any way.

Ian then said, "Helen this is everything you have been fighting for, this time he will and should get a whole life sentence, we wouldn't be where we are today without a good part of your hard work Helen."

I asked Ian, "what Mark Shirley's reaction is this time,"

He said, "Helen when I interviewed him he showed know emotions at all he just made a comment like why are all these women saying these things about me," "so Ian".

I said, "He's just denying it again,."

Ian replied, "Yes Helen he is but we have too much against him this time Helen so he will go to Broadmoor prison this time for life meaning life."

Liz said, "Helen are you alright"

I just replied, "Yes," as I really didn't know how I felt.

Ian then asked me if I would be willing to be re-interviewed under camera at the station, so I could tell them of any possible victim that

Shirley may of told me about on the day he attacked me. I did agree to the interview as I felt at long last it's now my chance of telling the police of the other angels i.e. victims if there true.

I have put a copy of the letter Ian gave me for you all to share and read, which states I would be prosecuted if I were to do any media work.

I have been visited by the Police today and have been informed that Kenneth Mark SHIRLEY has been recently charged with serious Sexual offences, these are historic and pre-date the offences committed against me, but only reported this year.

I understand that I have been advised not to publish anything about my case, do any interviews with the press and broadcasting companies such as radio and television, until after the trial, as it may prejudice and stop any trial against SHIRLEY.

It has been explained to me that if I do so, I will seriously damage the prospect of a conviction against SHIRLEY, and potentially stop any court trial.

I understand that if I disregard this advice I would be in contempt of court, and could be prosecuted.

SHIRLEY'S defence team will be closely monitoring the media, and will use articles to claim that he will be unable to have a fair trial.

Ian and Liz said they would contact me early January to make arrangements for the interview.

I replied, "yes ok," Ian shook my hand on leaving.

Liz said, "I will be in touch soon Helen,"

"Ok thanks Liz", I replied.

When they left the house I just sat for a while looking at the piece of paper Ian had given me, it's very hard to explain how I felt as there was a very big part of me that felt numb like I was in a dream and another part of me that felt sick and ill.

I was just sat on my sofa going over in my mind what Ian had just told me.

I did feel shocked as I had spent a long time convincing myself that these other victims of Shirley's weren't true, as I'd made myself believe for a long time that Shirley was just trying to scare me more on that horrible day. But in my heart even though I would tucked these victims away mentally, there has always been the thought of not knowing if any of them were true.

I started thinking of poor Mary Wainwright's family. I felt so sad and guilty for them as they have been through so much with the attack on myself and CID having to inform them after all those years that Shirley has re-offended and now this.

I thought it's terrible for them, I started thinking if only I hadn't of kept fighting for what I thought was right this might not be happening now for them.

It felt like Shirley had the upper hand again over me and mentally I could hear him laughing and howling about his victims.

I could feel in my inner self him dressing me, as for Richard I really didn't think he knew what to say to me, especially with our house being sold. He did say if CID had come out to us sooner he would of waited with the sale of the house.

As the days started to pass I started to struggle, I felt very low I kept going over everything i.e. the other victims Mark Shirley had used my body for. I felt very guilty as back in 2009 apart from saying there's more victims I never had the courage to tell my full attack and I've always felt CID didn't give me enough time, everything leading up to my trial felt so rushed and it always seemed to be about what happened to Mary.

I wasn't allowed to have counseling to tell the whole day as I was told firmly I had to stay pure for court, but I did piece in writing all the victims down in a writing book but over time I've trained my brain in thinking they weren't true apart from poor Mary!

It's very hard for me now as I now know at least one of them is true. Getting over new year was horrible we had to do our best for the children. Richard took the children bowling New Year's eve I stayed home as I felt very low and for once I just wanted some time on my own, as scared as I felt home alone I just spent most of the evening in floods of tears this was the first time in three years that Id managed to cry.

I went through my paper work with a very big sense of anger at the justice system every letter points out the same thing that the handling of Shirley was correct, I looked at the piece of paper that Ian had given me and for the first time in three years I recognized myself as being one of Shirley's victims. All this time over three long years I wouldn't allow myself to admit to my inner self that I was another one of Mark Shirley's victims.

I sat and cried thinking to myself all this time I've spent battling for other victims of his, so he wouldn't just be able to come out through parole again in the future to attack another women or to kill me or one of the others. I felt very upset and angry as here is a monster that has been allowed to attack women while all this time he was in the systems care i.e. on life license.

Everything that Mark Shirley put me through on the day of my attack now seems very real i.e. the other victims that Mark Shirley calls his angels.

I started to feel very angry with myself I need to tell Liz from CID everything, over the next few days I started to look at all the old notes I had made back in 2009, I put them all in order into a small folder including all the angel victims that I had just tucked away over time.

I got very upset over one small angel that Mark said he had killed if true I put her in my paperwork as the 10p girl.

On the 7th Jan 2012 I text Liz to find out when they wanted to interview me. I explained to Liz that I needed to tell her about the other victims, Liz text me back to say she would let me know on Monday and she also said, "Don't worry we can talk about everything when we meet."

On the 9th Jan I met with Ian and Liz at Thornbury police station at 10.30am, I really felt scared inside poor Richard was told he couldn't stay with me which crushed me a bit more.

I passed Ian the paperwork. I had on the other victims, plus I gave him parts of the missing chapter from my book which detailed parts of my attack and included Marks angels.

I gave Liz everything I needed to tell in the interview I had a few tears specially where I had to explain how he dressed me in different under clothes including my daughters, the interview was very hard for me as I don't know anything about this other lady as CID aren't allowed to tell me anything about her.

So me being re-interviewed by CID and telling them of these other victims if there true I don't know whether she's one of these victims or not.

After the interview I spoke with Ian about these possible victims, Ian said, "with what you have told us today Helen, I will have to pass this information over to the cold case team in Bristol to see if there's anything on file" plus Ian said he would have to send it to the cold case team in Wales again to see if there's anything on file.

"Ian", I said, "you will definitely alert Wales as the little ten pence girl has haunted me for three years now,"

Ian said, "Yes", "Helen I will get on it straight away."

Ian then said he wasn't sure at this stage whether they would need me as a witness for the trial he said he would let me know over the coming months Ian shook my hand and assured me he would keep me updated at all times and he would be in touch soon, "thank you Ian", I replied.

After the interview I felt very low and guilty it felt like I told all Shirley's dark secrets mentally it felt like I knew he would be very angry with me because on that horrible day he kept reassuring himself that I was a very trusted lady like Mary, the emotional effects of this was horrible.

A couple of days later my councilor lady came to see me we went over how all this has made me feel plus we went over all the nightmares that I've had over the three years. My councilor was very understanding we went over a lot of guilt that I was feeling for these possible victims especially the ten pence little girl.

Cathy said, "Helen if these victims are true you didn't hurt them Mark Shirley did, just like he hurt you none of you asked this man to do these things to you,"

I replied, "I know."

Cathy said, "Helen you were strong enough to survive on that horrific day and over time you have put all your strength into helping other victims and to make changes for others, plus you have been battling for what you feel is right also in hope of other victims coming forward,"

"I know", I replied I shared the paperwork of the possible other victims so Cathy could get a picture of how I pieced them all together she helped me understand that if the police were to find that the little ten pence victim is true at least her parents after all these years would know the truth and be able to put her to rest properly.

I cried but if it's true she's been out there all this time it's horrible Cathy! Cathy said, "Yes but it's not your fault Helen if its true Mark Shirley is to blame not you." I've only been seeing Cathy for a few months but she is very understanding and she's helped me a lot to put things into prospective mentally. Our work together always makes sense and I always manage to see things different, mentally it's hard to unravel things in my mind of that horrible day but at least I managed to put things back in the proper boxes in my mind with Cathy's help then I don't feel so weighted down emotionally.

# Mark's Secret Angels If True

## VICTIM ONE

### 1985- Ten pence Wasteland Girl

Shirley cried he was only 14years old, But she made him Angry. (Dead If True-Wales)

**Both innocent and pure but they made Shirley Angry.**

< ----------- >

## VICTIM TWO

### 1986- A Small Angel

He F\*\*KED her hard smelling her skin and hair, Again she made him Angry because she was only 15years old. He shouted her name, But can't remember. (Alive If True-Wales

## VICTIM THREE

### 1987- Mary Wainwright

Mary the trusted Angel. He told me how he killed her; He put her through a lot of pain. He just laughs and cries. (Mary's Death I Learnt Was True-Wales)

## VICTIM FOUR

### 2005-Mark's Silent Angel

Shirley shouted, saying you teased me for a few week's another pretty F\*\*\*ING Angel. He laughed saying he F\*\*\*ED and hurt her hard, she smelt sweet. This one won't tell, As I hurt and F\*\*\*ED her to hard, she's a sad sad Angel. (Alive If True-Bristol)

## VICTIM FIVE

**GIRL FRIENDS**

### Bristol area late at night

Walking home late after a night out with friend's, Shirley attacked another Angel from behind; he said she smelt nice, He was laughing because he had left her face down on the green and then ran. (Alive If True-Bristol)

In Between the Bristol area Angels, Shirley had two girlfriends Linda his main girlfriend, he laughed because he was crawl to her. And Cathy the girlfriend Behind Linda's back, she pulled on Mark's heart strings with another man.

## VICTIM SIX

### Bristol area late at night

Again walking home late, he attacked another Angel from behind. Again he F\*\*\*ED her hard and left her face down. Telling Mary as he laughed and cried. They made me angry, my breath was on them, I told them not to move as I had a knife, he laughed and cried. When telling Mary, They weren't pure Angels.

## VICTIM SEVEN
### 20th March 2009

The trusted Angel just like Mary Wainwright. Held for 5 and half hours. In her own house and raped. (Alive and True-Bristol)

I text Liz on the 20th Jan to ask her if she could take the tracker of the old address as the new owner asked me if I could sort it out, Liz was very understanding and she dealt with the tracker very quick which was good as the new owner wasn't being very nice over the phone.

On the 23rd Jan 2012, I rang my probation liaison officer to see if there was anything to update as I had a letter to say no updates at this time. In Shirley's sentence which I found odd as there was no mention of these new charges.

When I spoke with Mrs Smith from probation she assured me she knew nothing, I had explained to her how the police had come out to me in December 2011 and how I had been re-interviewed by CID. I told her how CID had recharged Mark Shirley for sexual offences which were historic before my attack.

I haven't always got on well with Mrs Smith but for once I could hear in her voice that she honestly knew nothing of these new charges, she kept saying how sorry she was that she didn't have any knowledge of anything, I replied it's not your fault Sarah she asked me what support had been put in place for me,

I told her none. She said she was going to find out what support I might be able to have while this case is pending, she said, she would get back to me as soon as she could, "thank you", I replied, she said she was going to look into this matter straight away.

After talking to Mrs Smith I really felt that the system again aren't getting things right all these professionals are supposed to work together I didn't hear anything for a few days.....

On the 26th Jan Liz phoned me to say hi Helen how are things with you it's just a quick call to let you know that Mark Shirley is in Bristol crown court tomorrow via video link at 11am, Liz explained that it was just for case management, I asked Liz if it would be in the media at this stage as I was worried for myself and family.

She replied, "I don't know Helen but if it is we will let you know,"

"Ok thanks", I replied.

She then went on to say, "Helen if it does you know you're not to make a comment,"

I replied, "Yes I do know and wouldn't Liz as I don't feel well enough and I know it would affect the trial."

The night was very long it was horrible. I felt really low I couldn't sleep, it really felt like I was back to the beginning of everything just praying that they put a stop on media as I need to explain to the children properly I want them to hear it from me.

The following day went really long, it was very hard not knowing what was going on in the court room, and there was nothing on the news which was a blessing for me and the family.

Liz called me to say that the court went fine and could she come out to me on the 30th January 2012 in the evening to update me, we agreed for her to come at 8pm.

Richard agreed to take the children down to my mum's house so I could see Liz, I started to feel a bit panicy as I dont like being home alone.

When Liz arrived she said, "Gosh you have moved quite far out do you like it,"

I replied, "No I don't like it,"

She said, "How nice the house was"

I said, "It will do for now, but it is quite small up to our old house."

We started talking about how I was feeling, I told Liz that Id been working hard with my councilor.

Liz said that court was fine she explained that the media is on hold at the moment, "that's good Liz" I replied, I told Liz how I want to explain to my children in my own time as they have been through so much over the three years.

We had a chat about Richard and how he's feeling about it all, Liz I think like me we are both upset as all the professionals over time have said the handling of Mark Shirley has been correct they said my attack was just a one off mistake.

Liz then went on to say that there has been a meeting with probation and CID she said I can't update you about what was said in the meeting but it has been agreed that at the moment so there's no confusion you will come back under us at CID she handed me a letter from Sarah Smith, Liz said she asked me to hand deliver it to you and said she would see you Helen after Mark Shirley's trial.

I did say to Liz that it seems very unfair after all my meetings over two years that they are all now having new meetings where myself and the MP aren't allowed to be updated, Liz replied,

"I don't know you can take it up with Ian,"

She said, "So from now I'm again your CID liaison officer is that ok,"

I replied, "Yes that's fine so we both agreed if there was anything like updates we would contact each other."

Liz explained there was no news on the other victims yet, she said for the Bristol ones if there's anything on the police file they would visit them, but it would be their own choice if they wanted to come forward and the same for the Wales police.

I said to Liz "So what about the ten pence girl", she said "well it was paper files back then not computers so it might take longer but both teams have been informed."

I said to Liz "what the cold case teams", she replied "Is that what you call them Helen,"

I said, "No that's what Ian called them when he interviewed me," we then said our goodbyes. When Liz left I text Richard to come home with the children, I made myself a coffee and took my diazepam tablets. I sat down and went over what me and Liz had discussed.

I felt quite hurt and upset for the way Liz queried the cold case team; it also didn't feel nice how they have full control over me again. At the moment life is not my own again I thought I'm not allowed to do any campaigning, my Facebook and twitter is being watched, my book is on hold. All I'm left with is a letter from probation and a letter from Ian in December.

I couldn't help feeling that for three long years life has been terrible, I've lost everything including my own home (for what I thought.) They all knew the handling of Shirley was wrong not that they would admit it and now all this. My emotions are very low and I can't help feeling in my inner self that I just don't trust them to get it right this time.

Richard came back with the children; I had to put on a brave face. I settled the children in their beds, my eldest daughter Amy asked how it went I replied

"It was ok Amy nothing to worry about darling." I gave her a kiss and she went to bed. I sat down and explained things to Richard, he didn't look very happy with the update either. I think we are both thinking the same i.e. what mistakes are they going to make this time.

The following day I went to see my G.P as I just wasn't coping to well, she highered my tablets. I have again enclosed a copy of the probation letters, which I would like to share with you all as you continue to read my story.

*Helen Stockford*

Mrs H. Stockford,
34, Manor walk                                              Date: 12/01/2012

Dear Mrs Stockford,

Further to our telephone conversation today, we are pleased to continue to be of service to you. As agreed I will be looking into support services, beyond what you are able to access at present, which are best able to deliver specialist support for your particular needs. Although you have advised me, that at present you are in receipt of service by your counsellor, I would be very happy to make enquiries and if you wish, follow-up with any appropriate referrals on your behalf.

Also as we discussed I will be liasing with the police next week, so that I may be advised regarding any further developments. As you have advised me today, perhaps you might find that you are notified of progress, in this matter before I am, but it is important that all of us are clear on the communication channels and responsibilities and we will clarify this jointly with the Police as soon as possible. Again, I apologise in advance, if you find that causes you additional distress at what must be a very difficult and upsetting time for you and your family.

I have taken note of your new address, and I hope that the points raised in this letter are clear but if you would like any further clarification, please let me know.

Yours sincerely


S. Smith
Victim Liaison Officer

<u>Private - addressee only</u>
Mrs H. Stockford,
34, Manor Walk                    Date: 26<sup>th</sup> January, 2012-01-06

Dear Mrs Stockford,

Further to our last letter to you, I am writing to inform you about a decision made at the joint meeting between Avon and Somerset Trust and Avon and Somerset Police, held on Thursday 26<sup>th</sup> January, 2012.

As you will no doubt already have heard from the police, it has been decided that all pre-sentence information regarding the new allegations against K.S. will come to you via the police.

We are working closely with the police, and as we discussed, I confirmed that we will also continue to be of service to you, in line with your entitlement. I will contact you again at the next key stage of this sentence.

Kind regards


S. Smith
Victim Liaison Officer

The month of February seemed to go very long, apart from seeing my councilor once a week which was really hard for me I didn't really hear much from anybody (i.e.) CID. I spoke with Charlotte Leslie my MP who advised me that I had to contact Steven Webb who is the MP for Thornbury to ask him if he would very much mind if Charlotte could stay my acting MP even thou we had moved from Charlotte's area, when I spoke with him he seemed very nice he was very understanding and said he didn't mind me staying with Charlotte as she had done so much work on my behalf but he did say if we needed his support in anything just to let him know.

On the 22nd February I wrote to Crispin Blunt to update him of the new historic case, as Jane Saddon had sent me some information via email and I knew I couldn't support anything at the moment to help to make changes in the justice system. Family life seemed to be getting harder, we are still battling with the council but with no houses available, so I'm feeling very low and stressed we are just struggling.

Richard can't find work as I'm not able to be home alone as it terrifies me the rented house I really don't like we have problems with the boiler and the house is very damp the children are not settling very well.

I think they feel lost plus the house is very small to what they are used to living in, so much for trying to have a fresh start I keep thinking will life ever get any better.

As the weeks past things just seemed to be getting harder I get my low days where I just feel lost as over the last two years I've managed to stay as strong as possible for myself and other victims with all the battling of the system to make changes now I just feel like I'm sat under the system with no hope of doing anything at the moment as they can prosecute me so I'm really struggling with the fact that I'm just another one of Shirley's victims that has to be silent.

The only thing that's keeping me sane is the fact that I keep telling myself I'm doing this at the moment to help the other lady's historic trial.

# 10ᵗʰ *April 2012 Plea Hearing*

On the 10ᵗʰ April 2012 Mark Shirley was due to appear before Bristol crown court via video link for his plea hearing, as being a victim of Shirley's I felt that I needed to go to the court so I could hear for myself what the charges were and what his plea was going to be in my heart I knew he was going to go not guilty but I just wanted to be there to hear him say "not guilty" as even thou CID had informed me back in December that he had been re-charged I have know trust in the system and mentally.

I just needed to hear it all for myself.

As scared as I was Richard and my son Scott agreed to take me to court, on travelling down to the court I kept thinking to myself am I doing the right thing. When we got to the court we went up to court room ten and stood outside as we were a bit early, round about 9.45am Ian from CID arrived with a colleague. They looked a bit taken back at me being there, I explained to Ian as a victim I felt I needed to hear it all for myself rather than wait for him to update me I explained to Ian that mentally I just needed to hear Shirley's plea as I wasn't allowed to go to the plea in my case. Ian was ok about it he said he understood his partner didn't speak to me at all at this stage.

We were told to go through into the courtroom, God I really felt scared and sick. We sat to the left of the court room by the court door, Geoff Bennett the media man from my court case was in the court room he came over to me and my family and told us where to sit. He was very kind as I think we were all feeling a bit out of place.

Ian and his partner came in with the barrister about ten minutes after us, Ian and his partner sat in front of us. Ian turned around and said,

"Helen after this we will have to have a talk if that's ok", I replied, "Yes that's fine."

There were a few problems with getting the video link started. I just sat there thinking to myself am I going to be in trouble after this as they want to talk to me after. The plea hearing started Mark came up on the screen, God it was horrible after hearing three charges and Shirley saying not guilty.

I didn't really hear anymore as like in my trial everything became muffled and I couldn't bare to look at him on the screen. I just felt dizzy and very sick, after the hearing I was told by Richard that Shirley has seventeen new charges and he pleaded not guilty to them all. Ian and his partner took us all into a side room where I was told by Ian that what I had heard in today's plea hearing I wasn't to discuss with anyone including the women's name.

I replied, "I wouldn't Ian I only came today as I wanted to hear it for myself mentally," Ians partner then turned and said, "Yes but you need to understand Helen, this women has really suffered over 7 years and we have been working with her since February last year and she's not in a good way mentally," something snapped inside me and I replied, "what and you think I am", I turned to Ian and stated a victim only has to be attacked by Shirley over a couple of minutes and it changes their life, so no one needs to tell me.

I need to understand as I'm stood with nothing today because of that man plus physical and mentally I'm a mess, Ians partner was very abrupt and rude. He then went on to say that the historic lady don't know Shirley by his name she only refers to him with CID as the man, I made no comment as I felt to upset ill and very angry.

Coming back home from court I felt very wore out, as I don't like going out as I find it very exhausting mentally going to the plea hearing was far too much for me. It took me a few days to get over it and to calm down emotionally, as for Richard and Scott they were both disgusted and angry for the way CID had spoken to me.

I think they felt like I was treated like a nobody and what happened to me back in 2009 didn't matter, they were both very cross and upset.

As the days went on Richard explained the 17 charges and what sort of things they were going to use in the new trial (i.e.) Mary Wainwrights case my 2009 case and Marks bad character plus the new historic lady's information. I felt very pleased that this time round they were going to be using everything but I couldn't help feeling hurt and let down by the system because his bad character wasn't allowed to be used in my trial plus for two long years.

I've been battling the whole system over the bad handling of Shirley's bad character while he was out on license since 2003-2009 and no one wanted to admit the wrongs. Everyone had assured me while he was out on license Shirley was good and probation didn't have any course for concerns, so they just ticked there boxes at every meeting Shirley attended at probation. Plus I felt very upset and angry for the way Ian's partner had treated me after the plea hearing.

I also felt that Ian had lied to me when he came out in December with Liz to update me, mainly because after the plea hearing Ian's partner told me that this historic lady knew nothing of Mark Shirley she only refers to him with CID as being the man. So when Ian said she came forward because of the pen-pal story and her fear of being part of those letters as she has a family this can't be true.

Ian's partner also said she knows nothing of his past crimes, so now I'm left feeling which one out of the two CID officers is telling me the truth. Mentally I just wish they would stop hiding things and start being truthful.

Over the next few days I started to feel my inner strength, so I decided I needed to do something so I wrote a strong email to Crispin Blunt and started to do some paperwork. I kept thinking how I couldn't start giving up I had to stay strong, I've come this far I thought to myself, plus on the 16th April I received a letter from Crispin Blunt on reading this letter I found my strength I thought I'd lost.

I contacted Charlotte and told her that I had received a letter from Crispin Blunt, she asked me to email it across to her. Charlotte advised me to put a letter in writing to her for her then to be able to act on my behalf; we made arrangements to meet at her Bristol office on the 7th April 2012. Again I'm putting these letters in my story which I would like to share with you all as you continue to read my story. I've also included my letter back to Crispin Blunt, plus my letters to Charlotte Leslie so she could act on my behalf.

Mrs Helen Stockford
34, Manor Walk

16 April 2012

Dear Mrs Stockford,

### Mark Shirley – Further Serious Offence

Thank you for your letter of 22 February about the offender Mark Shirley, who has been charged with further serious offences. You ask for a full review into the handling of Mark Shirley's case and for a meeting with the Justice Secretary.

May I firstly say how pleased I was to have had the opportunity to meet you and your husband Richard last October, together with Charlotte Leslie MP. I have to say that I was very moved to hear first hand of the terrible ordeal which you endured. I also appreciated you kindly taking the time to tell me about your work to assist other victims of crime.

I do understand that learning about the further charges brought against Mark Shirley must have caused you considerable shock and distress. Due to the serious nature of these allegations, I have ensured that Avon and Somerset Probation Trust undertakes a further review of the management of Mr Shirley's license, but applying particular scrutiny to the period following his release from custody in October 2004 up to December 2005. I have asked for the review to be completed this month, and following receipt of the review, it will, as with all reviews completed in accordance with the Probation Serious Further Offence (SFO) Review process, be subjected to an independent quality assurance process by highly experienced operational staff seconded to the Offender Management and Public Protection Group in the National Offender Management Service. The period during which Mr Shirley is alleged to have committed the offences for which he will now stand trial was reviewed in the Trust's earlier SFO Review. However, if the subsequent Review identifies failings and deficiencies not yet uncovered, my officials will consider what further action is necessary to ensure that learning is embedded into the way in which offenders, and particularly life licensees, are supervised by the Trust.

I am sorry that neither I or the Justice Secretary are able to meet with you at this time. I did try to address all of your concerns as fully as I could in our October meeting, and I am sorry if you feel that there was insufficient time to raise all the issues you wished to discuss. However, if anything significant is revealed in the further review of the management of Mr Shirley that has a bearing on the commission of the horrific offence to which you were subjected, I will of course write to you.

You kindly offer your invaluable input as a victim of crime into any future consultations or reviews which the Government undertakes. You may be interested to know that consultations for a review into the future of probation services in England and Wales and on planned reforms to community sentences have just been announced. This represents a real opportunity to help shape the future and function of the probation service. It is important to get as many views as possible so If you would like to put your views across you may do so at **www.justice.gov.uk/consultations.** The consultation process will run until 22 June 2012.

I know that this must be an extremely difficult time for you and your family.

CRISPIN BLUNT

## My letter to Crispin Blunt

34, Manor Walk

24.4.12

Dear Crispin Blunt,

Thank you for your letter dated 16th April 2012, I have today written to Charlotte Leslie to as if she can offer me any support with the review's dated from 2003-2009, I've also asked Charlotte Leslie if she can offer me any support in using the (Freedom Of Information Act) which might entitle me to look at some of the reviews on the management of Mark Shirley. I would very much like to thank you for taking the time to look at the serious nature of these new allegations and for asking for a review from 2004-2005, but on reading your letter I very much disagree as I have been battling with the system for two years over the management of Mark Shirley from 2003-2009 plus the re-offending from his prison cell (i.e.) Pen- Pal 2011. Everyone including yourself has assured me that the management of Mark Shirley was correct, this now seems to be incorrect, on reading your letter I very much would hope you would agree a full open review dated from 2003-2012 where myself and Charlotte Leslie would be allowed to be part of this review, it very much saddens me to think again the door is closed on this review, this is why I have asked Charlotte Leslie for her support.

Kind Rgds

Helen Stockford

34, Manor Walk
24.4.12

Dear Charlotte Leslie,

I have sent you Crispin Blunt's letter dated 16th April 12, I'm writing to you today to ask you if you can support me in asking Crispin Blunt if he can possibly look at a review from 2003-2009 of the management of Mark Shirley's license as it reads in Crispin Blunt's letter that he has only asked for a review from 2004-2005. I feel this is very unfair as I have been battling the system for 2 yrs, (ie) Government, probation and Parole for all the wrongs in the management of Mark Shirley while out on a life lience in the community. Everybody has assured me over the two years that the management of Shirley was all in order. Can you please help me with the Freedom Of Information Act, as I feel now that it is my right to see in detail the reviews dated from 2003-2012 including the review which they had last Feb/March 2011 and the review Jan 2012, I also feel from a victim's view that this review now that Crispin Blunt has asked for myself and you should be very much involved, I don't feel this should be an internal review I feel this is unfair, can we also if your willing try and set up a meeting with Jan Saddon or maybe Julie Adams (ie) probation - parole where we can both attend so that they can bring us up to date with everything as their was a big conference in Jan in Probation which again I think we should both be updated.... I have cc this to Crispin Blunt.

Thank You
Helen Stockford

I also asked Charlotte Leslie if she could help me with the failings of the sun newspaper (ie) pen-pal story I had to put it all in letter form to enable Charlotte Leslie to act on my behalf.

34, Manor Walk

24.4.12

Dear Charlotte Leslie,

I'm writing to you today to ask you if your able to advise me if I have any rights in pursuing the Sun News Paper for the Pen-Pal story dated the 10th Feb 2011, which at the time caused me and my family great distress also these letters are now part of a new trial this July 2012, as Mark Shirley has to stand trial for a 3rd victim, I very much feel these letters when sold to the Sun News Paper should of been handed straight to the police and not gone to print, can you please offer any support to me on how I can pursue this issue.

Thank You

Helen Stockford

On Friday 27th April 2012 I met with Charlotte Leslie and her P.A at Westbury on trym office. I explained to Charlotte what has happened since December 2011 when CID came out to my home and updated me on the new historic charges that make Shirley has been charged with. I explained how I updated probation and how probation told me they weren't aware of any new charges.

I explained that the police and probation had had a conference early Jan 2012 where they decided that I'd be better coming back under CID while this trials pending. I gave Charlotte two letters from probation which states this information, we then discussed Crispin Blunt and the new letter he had sent me dated 16th April 2012, Charlotte said that she felt Crispin Blunt had done his best to meet with me as justice ministers don't really see victims.

I said I fully understand but in the letter he sent me it says that he has asked for a review on Mark Shirley dated October 2004 to December 2005. I told Charlotte these dates were wrong as Mark Shirley was released back in 2003, my battle over the last two years has been for a review on Mark Shirley from 2003 to 2009 which Crispin Blunt is aware of. Charlotte said true but she said she will write to him thanking him but also to remind him that he has the dates wrong she said she don't think he will be able to do anymore as a minister. We agreed in today's meeting that Charlotte would write to probation Julie Adams to try and arranged a meeting, so we can discuss these new issues and the mistakes they have made again.

We also agreed that she would write to the media complaints commissioners to report the sun newspaper for the harrowing pen-pal letters dated 10th Feb 2011 and the stress that it has caused, plus these letters are also now part of the new court case this July. We also agreed that she would look into the freedom of information act to see if we can obtain Mark Shirley's previous reviews, if this is not allowed then we have agreed that maybe we will be able to go and look at the information,

Charlottes P.A is dealing with all these things as we have to go by Charlottes diary, I also gave Charlotte a copy of the letter I have written to Crispin Blunt and also two letters to Charlotte just asking Charlotte to act on my behalf. Charlotte Leslie said she would do her best in helping me.

As the long weeks have passed there has been new updates from CID, I'm trying hard to stay as busy as I can even though it's very hard. My eldest daughter Amy is about to leave school so I've been dealing with all her revision and supporting her as much as possible, we have been searching online together for her prom dress. My little boy has just had his birthday, as hard as life is at the moment I'm trying very hard to catch up on lots of lost time with my children.

Richard is trying so hard to support me as much as he can. I think he is struggling to come to terms with the fact that we have to go through another trial for another victim. Plus he's angry at the way the system has lied over the 2 years, we both know we have a very big hill to climb again but we can't give up. As for the council we still haven't been allocated a house we just have to continue to bid on the home choice web site.

On the 10th may myself and the councilor had a very long talk; we both agreed that we still have a lot of life work to complete. She feels that she may need to make a referral to get me some more help and support in learning to go back out into the community without fear, plus I'm going to need some support in learning to stay indoors alone without fear, so Richard can go back to work because I only have seven sessions left with her to cover the life skills work we have both agreed to wait until after the July trial as I'm finding it very hard at the moment.

I know if I don't cope without the weekly sessions I just have to ring the office, this was a very hard decision to have to make but we both felt it's for the best at the moment.

Over the following week I decided to email Charlotte Leslies P.A to see if there was any update from the meeting I had with Charlotte Leslie on the 27th April 2012, I also asked if there was any correspondence that Charlotte might have sent to various people. Charlottes P.A sent an email back saying that she was just waiting to talk to Charlotte about the best way to approach the press complaints issue, she also said that she had another person in the office who is organizing a meeting with probation i.e.

Julie Adams she asked if I had a list of things to discuss as it may help to have a formal agenda for the meeting, she also sent me a copy of the letter dated 8th May 2012 that Charlotte Leslie had sent to Crispin Blunt. Again I have placed a copy of this letter in with my story for you all to read, I emailed the P.A back with two lists of failures one list was for probation and the other one was for the sun news paper I also thanked her for sending me a copy of Charlottes letter to Crispin Blunt.

Crispin Blunt MP
Parliamentary Under-Secretary of State for Justice
Ministry of Justice
102 Petty France
London

8th May 2012


Ref: Helen Stockford,

Thank you for your kind letter to my constituent, Helen Stockford. Your taking the time to meet her was greatly appreciated.

Mrs Stockford has asked me to forward to you a copy of her letter sent to you on the 24th April.

Mrs Stockford points out that there appears to me a mistake in the letter of the 16th April with the date of Mark Shirley's release from custody as this was in October 2003 not 2004, and therefore she questions the date of the review as being from 2004 and not from 2003, and asks whether it can therefore start from 2003.

Mrs Stockford also asks that the scrutiny should extend beyond 2005 to at least 2009, owing to the number of issues and questions over what occurred during this period, as well as the very unfortunate 'pen pal' revelations in the Sun, and how this occurred.

Thank you again for all your help to date on this horrible case, and I would be very grateful if you would consider this matter.


Charlotte Leslie MP

On the 11<sup>th</sup> June 2012 Charlotte Leslies P.A sent me a letter from Crispin Blunt dated 30<sup>th</sup> May 2012 outlining the review from 2003-2009, on reading this letter I just could not believe what I was reading again he's outlined that all parties did their jobs properly and they didn't feel Shirley was a risk in the community or in prison again. I have enclosed this letter as part of the story for which I would like to share with you all as you continue to read my story.

Charlotte Leslie MP
House of Commons
London
SW1A 0AA

30 May 2012

Dear Charlotte,

## Mark Shirley – Serious Further Offences

Thank you for your letter of 8 May, enclosing correspondence from your constituent, Mrs Helen Stockford about the offender Mark Shirley. I have noted her comments regarding the review of the management of Mr Shirley whilst he was subject to life license between 2003 and 2009 and the more recent 'pen pal' revelations that have appeared in a national newspaper. May I once again express my deepest sympathies to Mrs Stockford for the extremely traumatic experience which she endured at the hands or Mr Shirley and say that I continue to admire her bravery and determination to help other victims of crime.

Mrs Stockford asks, specifically, that the additional review into the management of Mr Shirley's case be dated from 2003, which she correctly points out as the date he was originally released from custody on license, up to 2012. In your letter, you state Mr Shirley was first released from custody in October 2003, but in fact this release took place in December of that year. I can confirm that the period from this offender's initial release from custody on 10 December 2003 up to April 2009, when he was charged with the very serious crimes for which he was subsequently convicted, was covered by the Serious Further Offence (SFO) Review that was completed by Avon and Somerset Probation Trust in late 2009. SFO reviews in line with national policy and procedure cover the entire period of the offender's supervision in the community up to the point where he is charged with a serious further offence and examine those actions taken by the supervising Probation Trust to manage the offender's risk of harm in the community over that period. This is with a particular view to help establish whether all reasonable steps were taken to manage risks and protect others. The first SFO review, after completion by Avon and Somerset Probation Trust, was subjected to independent scrutiny and quality assurance by experienced operational staff working at the Offender Management and Public Protection Group. This review found no serious failings in the management of Mr Shirley's life license over this period.

In my letter dated 16 April 2012 to Mrs Stockford, I outlined that, following Mark Shirley's being newly charged with further serious offences committed in November and December 2005, I had asked Avon and Somerset Probation Trust to undertake a further review, to pay particular attention to the period following his release from custody in October 2004 (this was after he had been recalled to custody following his initial release on 10 December 2003) and up to December 2005. This was partly as the offences that are alleged to have been committed during November and December 2005 had not come to light when the original SFO Review was conducted. This second review was designed to augment the SFO Review that was completed in 2009 by re-examining the period that led up to the 2005 offences. I can confirm that this has now been completed and subjected to independent scrutiny by operational staff seconded to the Offender Management and Public Protection Group.

This second review found that Mr Shirley's behaviour following the second release in 2004 gave no undue cause for concern during the supervision period that followed. There was no indication, however, that those probation officers involved in Mr Shirley's supervision were complacent about his apparent compliance with his license conditions, and the evidence presented in the SFO review indicates that his risk of harm was managed effectively during that specific period, as was found to be the case generally for the whole of the supervision period from 2003 to 2009. Of course, the management of offenders in the community is not a straightforward business and risk can never be eliminated totally. In this case, there was no evidence to indicate probation officers were, or should have been, aware the offender was planning further serious offending, or indeed that he had committed the offences, between 30 November 2005 and 12 December 2005.

Mrs Stockford asks about the incident reported in the press where Mr Shirley wrote a number of letters to a 'penpal' whilst he was a serving prisoner. HM Prison Rules allow restrictions and conditions to be placed on a prisoner's communications to the outside world and for the interception of communications by certain prisoners on the grounds of national security and in the interests of public safety, to prevent and detect crime. Mr Shirley would have been informed that his communications were subject to monitoring on account of his offence and this monitoring would have continued for as long as the prison governor considered it necessary and proportionate to do so. Decisions to continue or to stop monitoring a prisoner's communications, both letters and telephone calls, are made depending on the individual circumstances of the case, based on an assessment of risk. Each case of this nature is subject to regular review.

As regards the publication of correspondence from prisoners, Mr Shirley is prohibited from writing about his own crimes or past offending if it is intended for publication or broadcast (or if sent would be likely to be published or broadcast). The only exception to this is if the correspondence consists of serious representations about a miscarriage of justice or forms part of a serious comment about crime, the processes of justice or the penal system. Although prisoners do not need prior permission to contact the media through correspondence, the above restriction would still apply.

Staff at HMP Bristol were not aware that these letters had been sent until they were published in the newspapers and were, therefore, not able to notify Mrs Stockford's Victim Liaison Officer about them and the likelihood of publication. I can only say how very sorry I am for the distress this has caused to Mrs Stockford.

There have now been two specific reviews into the supervision of Mr Shirley which together have covered the period from the time he was first released from custody in 2003 up to April 2009. Whilst I understand Mrs Stockford's concern that every strand of learning from this case be identified for the management of future cases, I am not persuaded that any further review into this period would be likely to uncover any new information. I can assure you that both reviews were taken very seriously by both Avon and Somerset Probation Trust and the National Offender Management Service and did ensure the each review involved close scrutiny of tha management of Mr Shirley's life license up to 2009.

I understand that the police in Avon and Somerset are keeping Mrs Stockford informed of the progress of the current court case.


CRISPIN BLUNT


As the weeks got harder and harder, inside I was feeling very low. My daughter Amy is home on study leave she's such a great daughter she's really keeping my spirit high, lots of fun with her prom dress. The first one we ordered off the internet it looked pretty online, but when I came through the post well it was terrible, five days until prom. We looked at each other we didn't know whether to laugh or cry.

Lucky for us we had Richards mum over from Germany at the time. We both took Amy to a dress shop where she chose such a beautiful dress, she looked so beautiful in it she had such a smile on her face it really touched my heart. Three years ago she was my little girl that was still at school now she's stood in front of me in this lovely dress an she is a young women, time had just passed so quick I thought. I couldn't help feeling sad inside as I can't bring those three years back but what I did think to myself on looking at Amy is she has been so brave over time and she's been very full of love and support.

We are very close and that has never changed. Richards mum and me shared the price of the dress, I was very grateful to Richards mother as this was the first time over the three years that a family member had helped us apart from my dad in the beginning.

On Monday the 18th June 2012 I felt a bit silly in front of Richards mother as we had to explain that CID were coming out to see me, she was very understanding she said she would go shopping with Amy and Richard.

This was very hard for me as I really wanted Richards support with CID but I agreed as she didn't know her way around the area. When CID arrived we discussed a lot of things e.g. the plea hearing I attended on 10th April 2012 we also discussed the new trial which is dated 9th July 2012.

Ian was suggesting that I only go to the trial for the verdict and the sentencing as she said he felt this trial would be too much for me, he also promised that he would update me daily from court. I felt unsure on talking to him as in my heart I knew I really wanted to go to court to see if I can put some sort of closure on what's happened to me and why Mark Shirley is such a monster. So I told Ian I would think over things and let him know in a few weeks' time. Ian said that was fine, we also discussed Mark Shirley's ex partner Cathy as they are bringing all what happened to me back into the trial.

I explained to Ian that Cathy Marks ex-partner had taken the two weeks of work for the new trial. I asked if she could be stopped as I didn't like the fact that in my trial I learnt that she had read the pathology report on Mary Wainwright and more when Mark Shirley was awaiting a parole hearing, Ian said, "Helen it's an open crown court where we don't think we can stop her from attending." He said, "He was due to meet the barrister so he would ask." "I felt really hurt by this as I don't think she has the right to be there especially with the fact that she told lies at the parole board hearing which helped his release in 2008 before Shirley attacked me."

We said our goodbyes Ian said he would be in touch soon, when they left I couldn't help having a few tears there was no justice for myself and Mary's family. The rest of the day and evening was really hard for me but I had to carry on and smile for the sake of my children and Richards mother. The following day was Richards birthday his mum arranged to take him out for a birthday meal with the children and me, it was a really nice afternoon out a real treat for the children as we don't do much as a family as we can't afford too. When we got back Richards mother was getting all her things together ready to leave as she had made plans to visit her other grandchildren, on thanking her for her help with Amy's dress and a great couple of days my phone rang. It was Ian from CID to update me, he explained that him and the barrister has been to court today and that the trial date had been put back to September I asked him why and he said he couldn't go into detail but it was something to do with Shirley's side.

He said when they confirm a date he would update me, he also said that he can't stop Cathy from going to court, I didn't get a chance to say goodbye to Richards mum I was too upset. Again I just felt like nobody to CID as it was only yesterday that they came out to me and there was no mention of court, I really felt let down again another long hard few months ahead of me. I just want it to be over (September with no date) gosh this is going to be hard I thought.

At long last Prom day 27th June 2012 has arrived for my daughter Amy and Cathy's Daughter. I promised myself I would take the pace of staying friends with Cathy until this final day for the sake of our daughters.

We agreed for Amy to meet at Cathy's house, it was heart breaking really for myself as our old family home was next door. Amy sat on our old door step and had some photos taken with Cathy's daughter. We took the girls up to Cribbs Casueway to get there limo.

Both girls looked beautiful, it was a brave smile from me for both of them, but inside my heart was broken. Cathy had a new partner with her, it was very hard we had a meal together and I said, "I didn't feel well," so we said our goodbyes and left.

I knew deep in my heart that the friendship was now at long last finished and the dark secret would never be told. I would never have to see Cathy again, but in my heart at least I knew both daughters had got through school together and now together with their friends at prom! I felt so proud of both girls.

Over the next few weeks life just seemed to get harder and harder. I'm trying to get on with everyday things for Richard and the children, but this trial was on my mind all the time.

Plus the fear of Cathy Smith learning of another victim's information was killing me deep down inside me. I kept thinking with all the mistakes made so far and all the fighting I've done over the two years especially with the lies told on the parole board and the knowledge of learning in my court case that Cathy had paper work of Mary Wainwright, surely this women wouldn't be allowed to sit through this victim's trial.

I texted Liz and asked if I could have a meeting with her and Will White, as Will White was the one that dealt with my 2009 case. Plus Will White had been involved in the January meeting this year with probation where is as decided that I would come back under CID and not probation until after this new historic trial has ended.

Liz agreed a meeting. On Monday the 16th July I met with Liz and Will White. During the meeting Will asked me how things had been over the two years. I replied it's been very hard but as a family we are still trying hard.

He asked me how I felt with CID coming back out to me about this historic case. I replied, "I wasn't shocked Will, but I'm very disappointed with the justice system." We went on the discuss why wanted this meeting, I explained to Will White how I had asked if Cathy Smith could be stopped from going to this victims trial as I felt she had no rights to be there considering the past history of the parole board and the lies that were told at the parole hearing.

I explained to him that CID had said they can't stop her from going to court in September as it's an open court case. I told Will White how unfair I thought this was and how upset I felt that Cathy had this right. I asked Will if there was anything legal that could be put in place to stop her from going to this historic case especially as they were going to use parts of my 2009 case as the bad character. Will White replied, "No Helen as it's an open court case," I replied, "well it really hurts me Will to think there isn't any justice for me or Mary Wainwrights family."

Will asked me if I was going to the trial, I said, "Yes I am as I need to try and fill some gaps from the day Shirley attacked me." Will said he would see if this was allowed and see what support could be put in place for me to attend. Liz my family liaison officer said she could check with her new boss and ask if she can come to the trial with me. I thanks Will and Liz for seeing me, Liz said, "She would call me once Will has checked things out." "Ok thank you," I replied. When I explained it to Richard he was feeling very much like me, but he was angry with the system. As the weeks passed by things were very hard.

We were still bidding on council houses as out private tenancy is coming to an end lots of pressure, mentally I'm beginning to feel very wore out, when is this ever going to end I kept thinking.

On the 7th August 2012 at 8pm I got a call from Liz my liaison officer. "Hi Helen how's things?" "Ok thank thanks," I replied, "just a quick call Helen," "Will has checked everything for you and yes you are allowed to go to the trial." "Ok," I replied, Liz then said, "but Helen I can't do the trial with you as my boss won't allow me the time off," (my heart sank to my feet thinking, "oh God I don't know if I can go without the support of Liz") I replied, "ok Liz don't worry but thank you for trying." Liz said, "Helen you are allowed to stay in witness care if you want to for support." She also confirmed the 11th September for the trial to start. We both agreed to talk son and said our goodbyes.

Later In the evening when the children were settled and in bed I told Richard that Liz wasn't allowed to come to the historic trial as her boss could not spare her for those two weeks. I also told him that they couldn't stop Cathy going to the court. Richard was very cross at this, I think he felt that it was very injustice of the system. He held me and said, "I will make sure she doesn't go for your sake Helen."

As a family we tried hard to enjoy the rest of the summer school holidays, we didn't do much as money was very short. Richard took our son Sam swimming a few times and Amy and Molly spent most of their time with me, my daughter Molly has a funny sense of humour so she kept me and Amy very amused. I think that's what I love most of all about my children they always make me laugh even through hard times.

When the children went back to school early September. Richard and my mother went round to visit Cathy; they both told her politely that I wasn't coping very well with everything including the new trial that was pending, so they ask Cathy to stay away from the court hearing as they both reminded Cathy that it had nothing to do with her and for my sake to stay away.

Cathy wasn't very happy but she did agree with my husband and mother. I will be honest with the dark secret that I've been holding I was very relieved to hear that she was staying away from the court trial, as I knew in my heart I wouldn't take the pace of anything if Cathy were there. I've managed to cut Cathy out of my life since the prom for our daughters. It was very hard waiting to get our girls to the prom. I thought to myself but I did achieve it without anyone noticing the dark dirty secret I held inside me with Cathy's full control over me.

# THE NEW HISTORIC TRIAL
# FOR MARK SHIRLEY

On the 11th September 2012 the new historic trial was due to start.

Not having much sleep the night before I felt quite wore out mentally. Emotionally I felt low. I knew in my heart it was going to be a very hard long day at court. As much as I felt I needed to be there, I was very scared about going into the court room knowing Shirley was going to be there. I kept thinking gosh why am I putting myself through this. It was a very strange feeling mentally I needed to know if it was true, was there really another living victim. I kept thinking surely he hasn't done this to another. It was very hard to think another woman had been terrified and hurt by Shirley! I kept saying to myself ("why wasn't Mary and myself enough"). It was also very hard for me as CID said, "This victim was before my attack." So there was a big part of me that felt ashamed in case she was one of the victims that he had dressed me like and tantrumed over the day he attacked me.

I managed to see my children off to school, they looked worried but I ashored them it was going to be ok. I felt so sad for them as they have been through so much. Gosh after getting myself dressed and taking my medication it was time to leave. The mood was sort of silent between me and Richard. We picked up our son Scott up on the way, I really didn't want Scott to come to court but he was adamant he wanted to come Scott looked very ill and pale. He so much wanted to show me his support bless him, I was so worried about him and Richard. On parking the car and walking down to the court I felt so dizzy and sick. Gosh I felt really unsteady on my feet, but I kept telling myself I needed to do this as part of trying to put some closure. Also to try and understand what type of person Shirley is, as my attack has left me feeling so confused.

When we arrived at Bristol Crown Court going through the doors again it felt like the time had stopped. It was like I had a heart beat that was thumping through me that didn't want to stop. We went through security and up to the second level; everyone was waiting e.g. CID, Media workers and the two barristers. It felt like we were sat outside the court room door for long time just waiting to go in. When we were told we could go into the court my legs felt so heavy, we sat down in the gallery every one treated me so nice. They all made me feel like it was ok to be there. Rosie Collins the barrister for my trial was dealing with this historic trial, plus there was another barrister working with her. All the professionals including myself and my family decided it would be better if I were to sit in the top gallery away from the jury. I was relieved by this as I wasn't going to take the pace of sitting in the main court room, sitting above was better for me plus it meant I could take breaks if things got too much for me.

The court case started with the victim barrister opening of the case. September 11th 2012, Mark Shirley now 42 convicted of raping yet another women in her own home. He's charged with 16 counts of rape and false imprisonment yet another attack which Mark Shirley denies; the attack had taken place in December 2005. I sat in the top gallery not knowing what I was about to hear, my legs wouldn't stop shaking as I listened. The barrister told the judge and the jury how the victim had briefly chatted to Mark Shirley in a pub by the waterfront in Bristol. He asked her lots of questions, gleaning where she lived. Three weeks later in December 2005, he burst into to her home wearing a balaclava and subjected her to a brutal and prolonged sex attack. During the attack he removed his balaclava and the victim recognised him as the man she'd met at the Bristol bar three weeks earlier. Gripping Richards hand I started to struggle to listen, but I knew mentally I had to stay however hard.

The barrister started to tell the court that during the attack he stabbed her twice in the stomach and he told her he would put 2p pieces in the holes. He started singing 'Mary Mary quite contrary' he also said "he hadn't a pretty knife for her". As the court heard the details unfold, I was struggling to stay composed, as the 'Mary Mary quite contrary' song gripped me.

Trying hard to listen my heart pounding and wiping away tears I couldn't help feeling my heart goes out to this poor victim. The pain and terror he had put her through I knew all about too. The barrister told the court even though this attack happened in December 2005; the victim had been too terrified to officially report it to the police until May 2011.

We listen to how the victim clean herself and her home and treated her own wounds herself, so her flat mate wouldn't notice. The victim was in fulltime employment at the time and tried hard to stay in work, but as time passed she didn't cope, she was seen by the mental health which over time helped her to report this terrible crime. The barrister told the court how Mark Shirley has killed Mary Wainwright in 1987.

The whole experience was getting very hard for me to listen too. The court listen as the prosecution barrister brought up details of my own court case in 2009, telling jurors it was beyond realms of coincidence that a different man could have committed such a similar offences in such a distinctive way. There were those peculiar hallmarks to his behaviour, the use of the blade and fascination for blood and least the reference to Mary and 2p coins.

The prosecution barrister said the similarities between the 2009 case could not be ignored, among other things.

Over the couple of weeks the court case was dreadful, it took me down very low listening to the victim via video link was very hard for me to watch.

I think with the fear of Shirley behind the glass kept me in my seat. He showed no remorse for the victim as she struggled through. Everyday got harder and harder, it was very hard as outside the court case I had to try and take the pace of normal life round the children.

I didn't want them to notice that there mother was struggling. I was very worried about my son Scott as he didn't take the pace of the court after the first day he was far too low to come. The only thing that wasn't stressful for me, Cathy Smith hadn't come to the court so far, if she were to come I know mentally and emotionally I wouldn't cope.

Even though the days seemed very long at court and it seem very hard. Mentally I've managed to understand things more, mainly because since March 2009 I always blamed myself like most victims, where we all think we should have done more to stop him.

But I looked at Shirley in the court sat behind the glass he declined going on the stand to try and defend himself; he looks so evil and nasty. I couldn't help thinking, "how many more women must suffer at this maniacs hands."

Verdict day 17ᵗʰ September 2012, gosh I have been dreading this part of the trial. I couldn't help thinking about the 2005 victim and how she must be feeling. I'm just praying they punish him properly this time. Kissing my children goodbye for school, me and Richard headed to the court the tension between us was quite low.

I think we were both feeling very wore out. When we got to the court we went straight up to the top gallery. The barrister and CID were sat in the court.

To my shock and dismay Cathy Smith, her boyfriend and her friend Sally walked into the court room. I felt sick to my stomach, I felt very angry with her as I didn't feel her and her friends had any right to be there.

My husband Richard didn't know what to say to me, he went down and spoke with CID but there was nothing they could do as it was an open court. I noticed Cathy get up off her seat, I was that angry with her, especially with the dark secret I still hold within me. I met her in the ladies toilets and asked her what she thought she was doing by being here at the court.

She said she couldn't stay away, she said she tried but she needed to know what was happening to Mark. I felt that angry I walked away thinking she should be ashamed of herself. Especially with what happened to me, her so called friend in 2009.

Richard sat in the main court room for the verdict as I sat in the top gallery with the 2005 victim. It felt very strange saying hello to one another. I did say to her do you mind me sitting here and she replied not at all, you have as much of a right to be here like me. So as strange as it sounds we both sat together and listened to the verdict.

The mood between us when they counted out 16 guilty was very emotional as we watched Shirley keep his head down; he just looked to the floor.

The judge gave his speech, which was outlined very fair he also added the punishment and told Shirley he could even possibly die in prison. Mark Shirley was given 16 life sentences with a minimum of 16years to serve.

He ordered Shirley to be taken down. At long last I knew that Shirley was going through the court door with the prison officers.

As I didn't watch this at my 2009 trial as mentally I had blocked it out. Myself and the 2005 victim gave each other a hug, I gave her my contact details and we said our goodbyes. She like myself is just an ordinary woman which Mark Shirley has destroyed.

**Convicted murderer 'broke into a woman's home and raped her for 12 HOURS after she spurned his advances in repeat of attack he carried out 18 years before'**

- Mark Shirley, 42, is accused of breaking into the woman's house in Bristol and repeatedly raping and stabbing her in an ordeal lasting 12 hours
- Shirley was out of prison on license after being convicted of murdering a 67-year-old widow in 1987 when the alleged attack took place in 2005
- The 'terrified' victim waited years to report the rape because she was afraid her attacker would <u>target</u> her again

By <u>Cathy Mcdermott</u>

**PUBLISHED:** 21:15, 18 September 2012 | **UPDATED:** 11:44, 19 September 2012

**Accused: Convicted murderer Mark Shirley, 42, is alleged to have raped and tortured a woman in a 12-hour attack with echoes of his other crimes**

A convicted murderer out on license broke into a woman's home and subjected her to a horrifying 12-hour rape ordeal - in a chilling copycat of his first attack 18 years earlier, a court heard.

Mark Shirley, who is alleged to have targeted the now 39-year-old after she spurned his advances in a bar, was said to have burst into her home wearing a balaclava 'like a scene from a horror film'.

He then tied her to her <u>bed</u> before repeatedly raping her at knifepoint and stabbing her in the legs over a 12-hour period, Bristol Crown Court was told.

The woman <u>claimed</u> Shirley, 42, even took breaks during the attack to make cups of tea, and sang the nursery rhyme Mary, Mary, Quite Contrary as he busied himself in her kitchen.

The jury was told that before Shirley left his victim's home he said: 'If you ever have sex again, you will only think of me.'

His alleged victim says she was left so <u>traumatised</u> by the 2005 ordeal she did not report it to police for six years.

In the meantime Shirley was convicted of a separate copycat rape - this time of mum-of-five Helen Stockford, at her home in Bristol in 2009.

Miss Stockford, then 40, was subjected to a terrifying ordeal lasting three-and-a-half hours in an apparent attempt to recreate the murder he had carried out 22 years earlier.

Shirley was convicted of rape and false imprisonment and was given a second life sentence with a minimum <u>tariff</u> of nine years, which he is still currently serving.

It followed his first conviction as a 17-year-old in 1987 for the sexually violent and ritualistic murder of of Mary Wainwright, 67, at her home in Cardiff. Shirley was given a life sentence but released on license in 2003.

After the second conviction the victim of the alleged 2005 attack came <u>forward</u> and Shirley is now on trial for 12 charges of assault by penetration, four charges of rape and one of unlawful and malicious wounding.

The victim has said she was too frightened to report the attack earlier as she was 'terrified' Shirley would come <u>back</u> for her, and that she piled on weight in a deliberate attempt to change her appearance.

**Victim: Mother-of-five Helen Stockford waived her
right to anonymity and spoke out after the earlier
conviction of Mark Shirley for her rape in 2009**

William Mousley QC, prosecuting, told the court that Shirley and
the victim had met on a night out in Bristol three weeks before the attack.

He said that, in passing conversation, the woman told Shirley where
she lived and that her flatmate was going away in three weeks' time.

The conversation was then said to have turned sour, and the 39-year-
old woman swore at Shirley 'to get rid of him'.

'They had not parted on good terms on that occasion,' Mr Mousley
said.

'He was a relative stranger to her. When he turned up in her home she
was not expecting him.'

On the day of the alleged attack in December 2005 the woman was
at home when she saw a white van pull up in her driveway, and then a
balaclava-clad man burst into her house.

She told police: 'For a millisecond I thought it was somebody messing
about. He pushed me to the floor - I couldn't work out who it was. He
said, "You can't say no now".

'It was like a horror film. All I could hear was my heart in my head
going bang, bang, bang.'

The court heard that the attacker took off his balaclava and said: 'You recognise me now, don't you?'

The woman told police in her interview: 'He was almost spitting at me, he was so angry. It was like he was an animal, not a person. He told me if I shut my eyes he'll slit my throat.'

At this point, she added, she noticed he had a knife.

Murder scene: This image shows police officers at
Cardiff home of widow Mary Wainwright, 67, who
was murdered by Mark Shirley in 1987

**First attack: The flat where 67-year-old widow Mary
Wainwright was murdered in Cardiff, marked by an arrow**

The court heard that the attacker went outside to get a washing line, which he used to tie the woman to her bed before raping her.

The jury was told that the attack lasted 12 hours, during which time the attacker repeatedly raped the woman, tortured her with a knife, gagged her and stabbed her in the legs.

The court heard that at one point the man left the room to make himself a cup of tea.

The victim told police her attacker had said he wanted to put two pence pieces on the wounds he inflicted - in an echo of Shirley's first attack where he left two pence pieces on the body of his victim.

The jury was told that, since the 2005 attack, the woman's mental health deteriorated and she was subsequently admitted to a psychiatric hospital after being diagnosed with Post-Traumatic Stress Disorder and depression.

She has drastically changed her appearance because of her fears she would be targeted again by her attacker.

When asked by Shirley's defence barrister, Sally O'Neill QC, why she started self-harming after the incident, the woman said: 'I have tried to make the scars my own so it's not like he's made them, because that scares me. It's about trying to regain some control over my body.'

Shirley was arrested in July last year shortly after the woman reported the crime to police. He was charged in December.

He denies ever having met her, being in her home or being in the pub where they allegedly met.

**On trial: Mark Shirley is on trial at Bristol Crown Court for the rape of a now 39-year-old woman in 2005**

# PUTTING LIFE BACK TOGETHER AFTER THE HISTORIC TRIAL

Trying to put family life back to normal after the Historic Trial was very hard as I was feeling exhausted, mentally and physically.

I managed to do a small amount of media after the trial as I knew deep inside me that the other victim wouldn't be strong enough to name and shame Mark Shirley or the justice system so I did it for the both of us. I started with the local Bristol paper, then on the 28th September 2012 I did Daybreak plus I did all the local news like the BBC and Radio. I wrote letters to government as I still felt very strong that the system had let Shirley's victims down.

I couldn't help thinking from 2009 until 2012 the system has just given me excuses after excuses and they are still telling me the same thing that the handling of Mark Shirley was correct in all areas e.g. probation did their job properly when Shirley was in the community and yet he'd managed to commit a further two bad crimes and play the whole system where possible. In-between fighting the justice system family life was getting harder as our private housing tenancy was coming to an end so we were battling with the council for a house.

Lucky for us the council gave me a priority card to bid on houses, poor Richard he was on the computer daily bidding, as a family we were all praying as we didn't want to be homeless. I was feeling very stressed and terrified of where I might have to live next. Gosh how I kept thinking on how I would just like all this to be a bad dream as I so wanted to go back home to my old house, before March 2009 we were so happy there.

It's true in life you can feel you have everything and be really happy and then something can happen and your left empty with nothing like us.

But like Richard and my children say at least we have each other I think that's what gives me the strength each day to carry on.

On the 6ᵗʰ October 2012 we were given a council house it's not far from where we are renting it's a 3 bedroom house with a nice big garden. Over the weeks we were busy decorating which our children enjoyed. My husband and children seem to be settling in well, they have got friendly with the neighbours which is nice to see.

As for myself I'm struggling with fear, I'm finding it very hard to settle, we are in the country area even though Richard and the children our feeling more settled and they are making friends which I'm really happy to see at long last, I can't befriend the neighbours because of all the fears I hold inside me, it's very hard but I just can't trust people. Plus I struggle with talking to people since my attack it's really hard and horrible.

The family next door to us is really friendly and nice her children are friends with my children. They always invited me around but I just can't bring myself to go. This might sound stupid to others but after befriending Cathy and Mark and it ending in sheer terror I just can't bring myself to trusting anyone.

Richard and I have had plenty of arguments over me not joining in with the neighbours and at times he makes me feel really low as I know in myself the sheer fear I've got of people, but I also understand that Richard must feel embarrassed when he goes round to next door alone if their having a family party he goes mainly because our children want to join in. But this is something that I am trying to work hard on as I'm trying to get better but it is something that is going to take time which I understand. I also understand it's very hard for the people I love around me to understand its going to take time.

Richard has now started back to work even though he has his own reservation about it; I'm really trying hard to reassure him that I'm coping home alone. Richard sends me lots of texts throughout the day; I think it's his way of checking I'm ok at home.

I think this big step in life has been hard for us both. The first few months of Richard working were dreadful for me even though I wouldn't dare show my family. The day would start by seeing Richard off to work, getting my children out the door for School, work or college then closing my front door behind them and locking it was very hard for me. Most mornings I would just sit in my hallway up against the front door and cry with sheer fear of being home alone, I would just sit and watch the windows and doors.

As a few weeks passed I started thinking to myself 'you can't keep doing this to yourself Helen!' I started thinking through some homework my counsellor had given me and made myself a daily plan. My daily plan started with getting up early having myself a hot drink, telling myself that Richard and the children would be up soon and will be leaving the house.

I would take deep slow breaths and I would cut an orange in half, I would hide it away normally in my cupboard draw in the hallway always telling myself the orange is there for when they all leave the house. This too everyone must sound strange I know.

But on saying all my goodbyes to my family, closing and locking my front door with a deep breath I opened my draw, took out my orange. On sniffing my strong smelling orange I would tell myself that Shirley is not in my new house he's locked away in prison far away from me.

Slowly I managed to walk up my stairway into the first bedroom to make the bed and tidy around; every time I felt fear I would sniff my orange and remind myself that Shirley is locked up far away from me. I had a lot of fear when cleaning the bathroom and again I used the strong smell of the orange plus the mirror to look at myself and say 'No stop Helen, Shirley is not in this room or any room in your new house as he's locked up faraway in prison. So this is how I learnt to cope with being home alone I do get odd days but over all I use a lot of strong smelling things around the home which help me.

I also use a lot of homework from my counselling when I wash myself and over time this has helped me a lot, so I don't make my skin sore, I always use a strong smelling talcum powder on my skin so I can't smell Shirley. For anyone that might read my story please try any strong smelling things like oranges, perfumes or talcum powder as it really does help take different fears away. But always remember to do a proper daily routine and stick to that pattern if you can plus remind yourself the person that hurt you isn't there, so even though I hate being home alone I always make sure I get through every day as hard as it maybe. I do feel isolated as I can't bring myself to driving a car and it terrifies me to go out alone. Richard is always telling me to get back on the road but again it feels like my family

.en't feeling the fears I've got so again we do argue over this and there are times where I cry in private where I wish to myself I could be the person I used to be as my life felt fulfilled back then.

As time has gone by the house is all decorated and looking nice, I'm starting to feel like we are trying to put family life back together. My children are looking forward to Easter we are making plans to have a family day trip which is something that I haven't done in a few years.

As Richard has been taking our children out on his own over time because I struggle with going out. Plus we have planned to do the back garden and put a small patio area so we have some where to sit and the children can bring their friends over for Barbeques. In-between all this I'm waiting for replies from The Justice System, plus I'm waiting on a reply from The Sun News Paper for my complaint on the Pen-Pal story. So even though I still have this big hole inside me and I'm still battling for Justice, family life is starting to feel a bit better.

As a family we were all looking forward to the Easter break, my daughter Amy was helping me with a surprise birthday party for my other daughter Molly as she's turning sweet sixteen. We were planning the party for Easter Saturday evening; weeks before the Easter break we hired a hall and a disco.

The week leading up to the Easter break we were so busy rushing around for birthday things and decorations for the hall. We couldn't find a Easter chick cake anywhere, so laughing together Amy said "don't worry mum, we will make one." I looked at her and said "Amy darling its Easter Saturday tomorrow love we don't have much time." "Yes we do" she replied.

"Ok I said we will go out in the morning and get what we need." We agreed to go to 'Sugar and Spice' store in the morning as that would be the last thing to buy.

As the day went on we were very busy preparing party food. By now Molly found out about her party so she was all happy making sure her friends could come. The party went really well, this was the first time I felt like life was beginning to feel a lot more settled.

# MY TRUE FEELINGS ON HOW MY ATTACK HAS AFFECTED ME

Over the six years, life been harder than anyone can imagine. I once used to get up in the morning and see my husband off to work with a quick kiss telling him I love you. I would then do the children and see them off to work and school, and then I would do the house work. The rest of the day would be my own where I would normally take a bath or shower and relax.

I always like my hair to look good, I would always put a touch of make-up on my face, I always felt good about myself and then clothes I wore. Nowadays, I can't do this as Shirley has taken this away from me.

As a rape victim, I don't get up in the morning feeling good about myself I can't look down at myself without feeling pain of what this man has done to me apart from the constant washing my hair and body to wash all his filth away.

Emotionally he has taken everything away, gone are the days where I would do my hair and make-up and wear nice underclothes and clothes. He has taken away the joy of wearing different kinds of perfume the most I wear today is a simple deodorant and Johnson's powder after each wash. I use lots of powder as this helps me mentally to take Shirley's smell away.

My life with my family has been full of different changes I'm still very close to my family but it's not like it used to be, the first year of the attack was really hard on my husband and children they went through so much as you already read, I think it's been really hard for the children as they haven't had their mother as they once knew her. I'm unable to take my children walking to local

Parks and shops as I'm terrified I might get hurt whilst out there in the community this really upsets me as my little boy is not as close to me as ne used to be he looks confused and sad at times. My little boy was once a mummy's boy where I would do everything for him, but over the past six years his dad has done parks and things with him.

He does say on odd occasions, "please mum I want you to come to the park why has dad always got to take me on his own rather than upset him I would make an excuse," I always have tears once they had left for the park there has been a few times where I have tried to go but they have ended up bringing me straight back then they are all upset.

There have been lots of bad times where my daughters have wanted to go girly shopping like most teenagers but we have had to tell them no as we have no money coming in, only our benefits which just covers food shopping.

I do feel very hurt and sad for my children as they have always had a good up bringing where they have had good clothes, daytrips and holidays have always been good. I would take them swimming and to local parks and libraries my little boy would do afterschool clubs.

I would always do my hair and make-up with the girls and would play and dance around the house after School. Through one day of crime my children have suffered with no family or friends to help.

I look at them when they are asleep at night and wish life could be what it used to be for them and myself, in my heart I know I can't bring back the six years I feel I've lost with them.

As for my relationship with my husband Richard things have been really hard he's been the best husband any wife could want. He's been with me through everything. It's been very sad and hard on my husband as even now

He still doesn't really know what happened to me on the day of my attack. Richard has lost everything he had worked so hard for.

Over the six years he has been so strong even though I can see in his face how much he has suffered Richard has always been the type of person that works very hard and enjoys family life but everything in the twenty-four years that's been stressful Richard would normally not deal with as I was always the strong one and yet as much as he has struggled he has done his best in taking over both my role and his.

Our children didn't really see dad much with long working hours and Richard has said himself how much he didn't really know about his children and their needs. As for our relationship it has been really hard we are still a very close married couple but not in the same way as we use to be we move around each other in the home in a very different way since my attack if I'm in the bathroom Richard knows to stay downstairs if I'm getting changed in the bedroom again Richard knows not to come in.

If I'm preparing dinner for the family and don't hear them coming in to the kitchen I panic. It's very hard to try and understand but this is how Shirley left me.

The sad part for us is if we try and be intermit, Shirley's face is the only face I see and I panic, I normally sit in our bed and cry.

Richard will try and comfort me telling me its ok babe it doesn't matter we have years together, making love isn't everything in a marriage he is so gentle and understanding and yet there have been times where I have said:

"Richard why waste anymore of your life on me your young enough to find someone else and start again."

I feel so cruel sometimes because I know I can't be the wife I used to be, Richard will just look at me and say, "Helen why would I want to do that you're no different to me then you were before, we will get through this together."

There are ties where I have had bad nightmares when I turn on Richard in bed thinking for a moment that he's Mark Shirley, but again Richards understanding he will comfort me and reassure me that Shirley's locked u and not in the house.

My poor husband I look at him and think you have gone through so much over six years another man would have walked away just with the stress alone

I can't help thinking if I hadn't of befriended Cathy in the school playground this attack wouldn't have happened. I wish from the bottom of my heart now.

I had listened to friends and family for example my mother and sister, as they both said there was something about Cathy that they didn't like, my mother warned me time and time again she would say.

"Helen don't trust that one," I used to say, "mum your being silly There's nothing wrong with Cathy she's a good friend." At that time I didn't know what was around the corner too destroy a big part of my life.

But one thing I have learnt over time however hard it maybe to report a crime, six years on I wish I had of had the strength back in 2009 to of told the police the whole story. So for anyone that might read my story, remember if at any time in your life you need to report a crime however scared or distraught you may feel don't hold back tell the police everything.

The police are very good and very understanding. As for me I'm still trying hard to put life back together, I take one day at a time. I will always try to make changes in hope to help other victims and their families.

# A STRONG VOICE SPOKEN FROM THE HEART

I think for anyone, young or old, it should not matter whether you are male or female. If you have been attacked or you no someone that might of been, try and help them, believe me when I say there feeling very lonley, not knowing what to do or who to turn to for help, please for any grandmother or mother, sister, brother or even a close friend support that person.

Don't let them feel lonely and on there own like I did, everyone needs someone close; someone they can lean on and cry with. Someone to hold them, and tell them its going to be allright, dont look at a victim and think god they have changed, because believe me they haven't, they are still that same person deep down inside, so please support them xx

Printed in Great Britain
by Amazon

27577004R00131